The Art of Calm

The Art of Calm

Spiritual Exercises for the Anxious Soul

Roger Hutchison

Morehouse Publishing
NEW YORK

Unless otherwise noted, the Scripture quotations contained herein are from the New Revised Standard Version Bible, copyright © 1989 by the Division of Christian Education of the National Council of Churches of Christ in the U.S.A. Used by permission. All rights reserved.

Morehouse Publishing, 19 East 34th Street, New York, NY 10016

Morehouse Publishing is an imprint of Church Publishing Incorporated.

Cover design by David Baldeosingh Rotstein
Cover photograph by Anna OK / Shutterstock.com

Library of Congress Cataloging-in-Publication Data
Names: Hutchison, Roger, author.
Title: The art of calm : spiritual exercises for the anxious soul / Roger
    Hutchison.
Description: New York, NY : Morehouse Publishing, [2023]
Identifiers: LCCN 2022062155 (print) | LCCN 2022062156 (ebook) | ISBN
    9781640656321 (paperback) | ISBN 9781640656338 (epub)
Subjects: LCSH: Anxiety disorders—Religious aspects—Christianity. |
    Depression, Mental—Religious aspects—Christianity. | Art therapy. |
    Stress management. | Meditation.
Classification: LCC RC531 .H88 2023 (print) | LCC RC531 (ebook) | DDC
    616.85/22—dc23/eng/20230203
LC record available at https://lccn.loc.gov/2022062155
LC ebook record available at https://lccn.loc.gov/2022062156

For my mom and dad.
I love you.
—RH

CONTENTS

IMPORTANT MESSAGE FROM THE AUTHOR

THE ART OF CALM: SPIRITUAL EXERCISES FOR THE ANXIOUS SOUL FEATURES honest stories of my descent into fear and anxiety, a diagnosis of mental illness, and how I found my way back to a place of stability and health. I wrote it for those struggling with anxiety, fear, and panic. I hope my story and the practices I provide will inspire and encourage each of you.

The mental health information I provide is for general informational and educational purposes only and is not a substitute for professional advice. Accordingly, before taking any actions based upon such information, I encourage you to consult with the appropriate professionals. There's also a list of mental health resources in the back matter of this book.

If you're thinking about suicide, are worried about a friend or loved one, or would like emotional support, the Lifeline network is available 24/7 across the United States by dialing 988 now.

The Lifeline is available for everyone, is free, and confidential. Remember, you are not alone.

How to Use This Book

Whether you live with mental health issues, have family or friends that do, or are interested in learning more about mental health issues, one of the best ways to learn about mental health is through books written by people dealing with those issues every day.

It is my hope that *The Art of Calm: Spiritual Practices for the Anxious Soul* will help you encourage, support, and care for people dealing with mental health issues every day.

And that person might just be you.

NAMI, Mental Health America (MHA), and other national and international organizations say that talking about mental health not only increases your likelihood of getting support but helps in decreasing the stigma surrounding mental health.

This book is designed for both individuals as well as small groups that might include pastoral care groups, Bible studies, Sunday school classes, grief and loss groups, book clubs, classroom settings, therapist's offices, and more.

There are reflection questions, journaling prompts, and practices that will help individuals lead a more grounded and centered life. Practices ranging from photography, art, music, and meditation to cooking and hiking will hopefully help you reset your outlook and find yourself again amidst inner and outer turmoil.

SMALL GROUP USE

As mentioned above, these exercises can be for personal or group use. If you would like to use this book for a small group setting, be aware that organizing and maintaining a book study group takes intentionality, time, and effort.

My tendency is to help everyone. Don't put that pressure on yourself. The broader the group, the greater effort you will make to help others understand their similarities. You are not trying to fix anyone.

Fostering an atmosphere of respect will determine everyone's ability to share with one another. Individuals will have experiences that are uniquely their own. As facilitator, it is your job to model a spirit of respect. You might even want to invite a mental health professional to speak to the group. A professional can answer questions with expertise.

Although you may opt to hold support group meetings in your home, I recommend you seek out schools, colleges, churches, community centers, libraries, or other free space in your community. Regardless of the location, however, a well-organized marketing effort will prove invaluable to your group's success. Develop a flyer that briefly describes your group, where and when it meets, and contact information. You will also want to make sure you have the necessary supplies available for the different exercises and activities. Decide if there will be food or other refreshments. I do not recommend serving alcohol during the book study. You do not know how alcohol may impact someone who attends the meeting.

I encourage your group to focus on one chapter each week with each member invited to have a chance to share thoughts about it. Nobody should be forced to speak; it is always acceptable for someone to decline to respond.

A reminder about confidentiality: Anything of a personal nature that is shared is never repeated outside your group unless permission has been given. Commit to create a "safe place" where participants can share and experience life together. Agree to support each other by listening and encouraging one another. (Based on the ADAA's [Anxiety and Depression Association of America] Starting a Support Group: https://adaa.org/finding-help/getting-support /support-groups/start-support-group.)

INTRODUCTION

When I was in the seventh grade, I was voted "shyest" student in my junior high school. Not most likely to succeed. Not most athletic, or most likely to run a major corporation.

Everyone else saw my being reserved, nervous, or timid in the company of others as being shy. What they didn't see—or recognize—was that I was lonely. I was a daydreamer. I was creative. I was sensitive. I longed to be liked and wanted to have friends, even if making friends did not come easy for me.

And now those feelings were on full display for everyone else to see. I was shy—yes, but I was also lonely. Of course, what I didn't know then was that I was not the only person feeling that way. Who doesn't want to be liked? Who doesn't want to have friends? But that feeling of aloneness planted within me the seeds of anxiety, and panic had taken root in my soul. Over time, this emotional garden would impact my life in ways I could have never imagined.

Decades later, in the fall of 2017, I had an acute mental health episode and ended up in the emergency room—not once, but twice. I have never experienced such fear, sadness, or hopelessness. It was if I had lost my mind. And I felt very alone.

I am not alone. I am surrounded by amazing family and friends. I have a wife who saves my life every day. We have a daughter who teaches us about resilience and passion. I have colleagues and friends all around the world who know and love me: the shy me; the empathetic me; the sensitive me; the reactionary me; the creative me.

And still, my internal world unraveled, and I was left frayed and broken.

With the support and encouragement of family and friends, I began the hard work of learning to not only live with but also thrive in a world that isn't always user-friendly to those who struggle with mental illness. I received a diagnosis of Generalized Anxiety Disorder and ADHD (attention deficit hyperactivity disorder). I started medication. I learned different strategies to calm myself when anxiety crawled across my skin like an insect.

But anxiety is harder to swat away.

When Covid hit and day-to-day life as we know it was forever changed, I worried about how I was going to handle the fear, stress, anxiety, and the unknown. So much unknown.

I didn't feel good in my skin. I worried that all the inner and outer work that I had done to heal my soul and mind was for naught. My psychiatrist and therapist prescribed medication. They also prescribed exercise and outdoor activities. I've always had a love/hate relationship with exercise and my body. But I wanted to feel better, so I decided to give it a try.

In doing so, I discovered the healing power of moving my body. I discovered a special kind of yoga (just wait!), and I went for a walk. I put on my tennis shoes and walked around the block, and I began to pay attention to the world around me in a new and more intimate way.

I love color and design, light and shadow. I wanted to remember the things I was seeing, so I began taking photographs with my phone. I took photos of flowers, bugs, fire hydrants, and birds. I especially enjoyed taking photos of the sidewalk.

I walked around the block each morning for several weeks. Then, a mile. Two miles. And by the time we were well into quarantine life, I was walking as many as six miles a day. I discovered that walking and photography pulled me out of the pit of fear that

I had fallen into. When I walked and when I was looking for things to photograph, a sense of calm would wash over me.

I felt centered and grounded for possibly the first time in my life.

In time, I purchased a better camera and started taking photographs of birds and other amazing creatures that I simply did not see moving in the world prior to quarantine and my mental health crash.

I've also made some incredible friendships out on the trail—like my friend Sr. Mary, a nun, school nurse, and amazing photographer. Not everyone I meet on the trail views life through the lens of faith, and although ours is different, Sr. Mary and I see the world in similar ways. We both strive to capture the holiness of the animal we are photographing. Photography has indeed helped me feel less alone.

I am now always finding new ways to see the world—not just looking but SEEING. In fact, it often feels like I'm experiencing the world as a child—not some jaded and stressed-out adult, but almost as a blind man given the gift of sight.

This is a book to help you, the reader, achieve a similar kind of clarity where there once was none.

It is a book that will hopefully encourage you or someone you love.

You are not alone.

Count me as a comrade.

A friend on the journey.

With anything we want to be good at or feel success with, we must practice. This applies to something as familiar as riding a bike. It also applies to finding peace and calm in your life.

For me, photography is a practice that makes me feel grounded. It gives me the ability to stay calm and connect to the core of who I am in moments of stress and uncertainty. You may discover that the language and act of making art helps you find a sense of peace. Maybe it is music, or writing. Maybe it is cooking, dancing, or singing. Maybe it is taking ten minutes a day and learning to breathe with intention and focus.

I encourage you to find whatever practice, or practices, work best for you, while also remembering that the benefits might be hard to see at first. So, give it time. Practice.

I promise it will be worth it.

I am honored you are here.

—Roger Hutchison

"I am seeking, I am striving, I am in it with all my heart."
—Vincent van Gogh,
The Letters of Vincent van Gogh
(Touchstone, repr. ed., 2008)

1. CRASH

Christ, be with me. Life is crashing down around me. Christ, be with me.

I WAS COLD. EVEN WITH SIX BLANKETS PILED ON ME, I WAS SHIVERING and could not get warm. I held the EMT's hand while in the ambulance. I worried that I was being too much trouble and kept apologizing. I always apologize.

Earlier that evening, my wife, Kristin, and our daughter, Riley, thought dinner out might cheer me up, so they took me to Cracker Barrel—one of my guilty pleasures. I ordered my favorite meal but could not eat it. One bite and I had to put my fork down. I looked across the table at the two people I love the most, and my vision began to blur so badly I literally couldn't see their faces. I was terrified, so we went home, and I climbed into my most comfortable chair when an overwhelming sense of doom overtook me. I couldn't catch my breath, and my heart felt like a grenade that had just had the pin removed. Awaiting the impending explosion brought me to hysterics.

Kristin called 911.

I latched on to my wife's hand once we were together in the ER. Her touch felt warm. It felt safe. It felt familiar.

I know her eyes. I observed them, and they looked tired. Red around the edges. I was a boat filling with water, and she kept me from sinking. I was holding on for dear life and unsure if I would stay afloat.

Kristin and I were married on June 6, 1996. We were both twenty-three years old. I wish it was more exciting, but we met at church. Her mom tried to set us up. "He's a nice boy. You should call him."

And she did. She left a message. And I waited a day or so. I didn't want to seem eager. But I could not have been more excited.

We ended up going on that date. It's been twenty-seven years now, and I love her more every day, even if relationships are never always easy.

Kristin's worries for me, and the countless other challenges we were facing—financial, parenting, work, and the daily barrage of hate-filled politics and division—had worn her down. It sounds extreme now, but at the time, she just wanted it all to be over. The memory haunts her still.

A couple of weeks before the night in the hospital, she thought the warm sunshine and the fresh air might help my mood. And she needed a break.

I started alone, made it as far as a bench across the street from our home, and frantically called her to come to sit with me. I couldn't handle being by myself.

She joined me, and like a young child, I put my head in her lap and began to cry. She remembers hearing a plane flying overhead and longed for it to crash into us.

"Death would be easier than this," she thought to herself.

It was all too much. It is too much. Cold fluid from a clear bag filled my veins. I began to shiver. More blankets. I looked and smelled like a basket of dirty laundry. The sounds and sights of the emergency room plowed through my head like a train. My arms burned, my heart raced, and my vision was foggy. And I was trying to devise a way to tell my daughter that I was dying.

I told Kristin I needed her to be in the room when we told our daughter I was dying. She just looked at me and then told me to close my eyes and get some rest.

So that's her way of telling me to shut the hell up.

My head was telling me I was dying, and my stomach was telling me I was dying. And WebMD was telling me I was dying. But I wasn't dying. I didn't have colon cancer—even though I had every indication of cancer based on certain symptoms listed online.

I could feel my heart beating in my chest, ears, and toes. The echocardiogram showed that my heart was healthy. I wasn't having a stroke, even though I told Kristin that my pupils were different sizes and my arm hurt.

God bless her.

I've since learned that I was in the throes of a prolonged panic attack and did not understand what was happening. It had taken control of my body, mind, and soul. And I had allowed it to do so. I have always been a worrier. My brain is on spin cycle—fixated on the what-ifs. I was spinning out of control—especially at night.

We purchased our home in early 2017. Hurricane Harvey made landfall south of us not long after we started to feel settled. The storm stalled above our community, bringing devastation and destruction to many.

In fact, it was a Category 4 hurricane before making landfall in Texas. Catastrophic flooding ensued and there were more than one hundred deaths. It is tied with 2005's Hurricane Katrina as the costliest storm on record, inflicting $125 billion (2017 USD) in damage, primarily in the Houston metropolitan area and Southeast Texas. In a four-day period, many areas received more than forty inches of rain as the system slowly meandered over the state and its adjacent waters. With peak accumulations of 60.58 inches, Harvey was also the wettest storm on record in the United States. More than thirty thousand people were displaced, and more than seventeen thousand rescues were attemped, not all successfully.[1]

Thankfully, we did not flood, but three weeks after the storm, while I was cooking eggs, I noticed that the eggs kept sliding to the left of the pan. I wondered if the stove needed balancing. The stove wasn't off-balance.

Our kitchen floor had dropped three inches. Cracks formed in our doorframes and walls. Our home's foundation was failing due to the ground saturation around and under our house. We also discovered that the plumbing under our home burst due to the sinking of the foundation.

At night I could hear cracking in our walls and dripping water. I would lie awake, wide-eyed. The moonlight, once comforting and peaceful, jeered at me through the blinds. I tried to close him out, but he always found his way into our room. If I dozed off, I would experience a sudden sensation of falling. It would startle me awake, my heart racing, my breath fast and shallow.

I *knew* that our house was going to collapse. By keeping watch, I was preparing to bear witness to the destruction I knew was coming.

I was not sleeping. I was not eating. And you are in big trouble if you aren't doing those two things. My foundation had failed me. Literally and figuratively.

The last straw came when our insurance company told us they wouldn't pay for the damage. None of it. I remember shouting at the poor person on the phone. We had been clients for over twenty-five years and maybe used the insurance once. That did not matter. Case closed.

And from my hospital bed, I felt my figurative foundation failing.

The first nurse I encountered in the ER put another IV in my arm. It didn't feel right, and I told her it was hurting. When the area around the needle started filling with blood, I knew it was a blowout. Kristin felt my hand grab tighter as the tears rolled down my face.

She patiently smiled at me.

I never promised that making space for calm in your life wouldn't take significant work and emotional investment. Soul work is difficult work. Important work often is.

It took years to look back at this traumatic night in an ambulance and the emergency room and not be triggered. Now, though, I can remember this moment in time as just that—a moment in time.

I have a friend who sat with me during a panic attack that hit while I was in my office at work. I will never forget her words. "Roger—just as I am sitting with you in this scary moment, you will one day sit with someone else who needs you." And she was right.

Please pull up a chair, and let's sit together. You are not alone.

INVITATION

I invite you to reflect on a moment when you felt like your world was crashing down. Maybe it was in your past. Maybe it is right now. Feel free to use words, drawings, collages, paintings, or other methods you would prefer to use as you engage with these questions.

Make sure you are in a safe space. Take a deep breath. Using crayons, colored pencils, paints, markers, chalk, or oil pastels, create a visual response inspired by this challenging moment in your life. It can be a drawing or painting. You can doodle or make a collage. Choose your colors with this in mind. Are your lines jagged and rough? Is the page full, or is there negative space?

You may experience intense emotions while working on this project. That is a good thing. Lean into those feelings.

Just remember to keep breathing.

If you need to take a break or put it away until you are in a better place, please do so.

REFLECTION

- How did you find yourself in this place?
- What were you feeling, and how were those feelings manifested?
- What color were these feelings?

SUPPLICATION

Christ, be with me. Life is crashing down around me.
Christ, be with me.
In my breathing.
Fast or slow.
Deep or shallow.
In my body and soul—such emptiness.
The flame is flickering—soon to go out.
I long for oxygen and transformation.
A longing for you.
You hold me.
You see me.
Touch me. Hold me.
Help me to know that when I am crashing down,
You are there.
Christ, be with me. Life is crashing down around me.
Christ, be with me.
Amen.

2. Rescue

Even in my lowest moments, I've found that I was not alone.

His name escapes me, but I will never forget his face and gentle act of kindness.

It was morning. I wouldn't have known this, except that Kristin had returned to the hospital after going home to get some rest. She also needed to be with our teenage daughter, who was worried about her daddy.

Other than some fluids, a busted vein, and an obscene medical bill, I received little else from my overnight stay in the emergency room. I wanted to feel better, and I didn't. I felt robbed and ignored, as if I had been left in the ditch to die.

Like the story of the Good Samaritan, beaten and bruised, I needed rescue. I needed someone to tend to my wounds, take my hand, and tell me that I would be OK.

When I shared this with the doctor, the first words out of his mouth were to ask me if I felt like harming myself. He asked if I was contemplating suicide or was a danger to myself or others.

I was not suicidal.

I was exhausted.

Broken.

Afraid.

Sad.

He told me that the only way he could get me immediate mental health care was for me to say to him that I was suicidal. Until then, there was very little he could do.

He quickly moved on to his next patient, whose wounds were visible.

The happy-hospital-bill lady rolled her computer/credit card machine in and had us sign some paperwork and pay a portion of the hospital bill. If I had not been so sick, I might not have been able to hold my tongue.

We have a broken medical system.

Someone else came in shortly afterward and handed us an impossibly large stack of paper that included instructions on how to find a therapist and psychiatrist. On top of the stack was a document I had to sign stating that I wasn't going to kill myself. For a brief second, I thought about not signing it. And then we were told we could go home.

To no one's surprise, I began to cry. Again. Not just a few tears, but a raging river of tears—desperation and anger like I had not felt before. Time for us to go home? I loved my home, but I didn't want to go home.

Home is where I would wake up in the middle of the night and hear the creaking and cracking of the walls. Home is where I wasn't eating. I wasn't sleeping. Home is where my pupils were of different sizes. Home is where I would stare into the toilet while looking at a color chart. Home is where the EMTs had to come to get me in the middle of the night—the neighbors peering out of their windows.

Home is where they loaded me on a stretcher. I was embarrassed that I was too heavy for them to carry and told them so. Even then, I was stressing out about how I looked and how much of a burden I was.

Home is where I was losing my mind.

And then he appeared.

I had seen him off and on through the night. He had checked in on me a few times.

The nurse who blew out my vein was gone, and this man was now at my bedside. Usually, I'm not particularly eager to make a scene, but I was *done.*

I cried out to him. I told him that I had come to the hospital because I wanted to feel better, and all I received was a terrible bruise and a stack of papers telling me how to find a therapist. I shouted that I had lost nearly thirty pounds in less than a month and knew I needed to eat but wasn't hungry. That I needed to sleep, but my mind wouldn't stop spinning. That I thought I was going crazy.

With the most gentle and caring bedside manner, he took my hand, looked at my wife and me, and told me that he had been watching me throughout the night and that even though it didn't feel like it now, I was going to be OK.

He was the first person I believed.

He shared with us that I reminded him of a soldier he once knew who had been to war. He recognized that I was exhausted. That I had fought until I couldn't fight anymore.

He said he knew all this because he was that soldier and had been in the same ditch as me.

He told us he didn't feel good about sending us home without something to help me feel better.

I still had a long road ahead, but he reached into that familiar ditch, pulled me to safety, bandaged my wounds, and asked the attending physician if he would prescribe something to help settle me and help me sleep.

The Good Samaritan wrote his phone number down on a piece of paper and told us that we could call him if we needed his help. He told us he didn't usually do this but felt a true kinship with me and wanted to help if he could. We never reached out.

Maybe I should now.

My tears, once raging, were now tears of gratitude. I felt less anxious. Less afraid. By the time we got to our car in the hospital parking lot, I was as relaxed as I had felt in months. Maybe years.

And I was finally hungry.

Kristin, sensing the opportunity to get some food in me, excitedly told me she would take me anywhere to get something. She knew what I wanted: a bacon, egg, and cheese biscuit from McDonald's, two of them—and a large orange juice and hashbrowns.

McDonald's was the first food I had eaten in over two weeks, and it felt like Thanksgiving dinner.

In many ways, it was.

———————

I connect the parable of the Good Samaritan to the man in the emergency room. Looking back at this experience, I can recognize the importance of asking for help when you can. Sometimes we are unaware that we need help, or we don't want to ask for help.

If you know someone like this, and you are able, please reach out to them. Extend a hand. Open your heart. And don't make any promises. Promises aren't needed.

Your presence is what is needed most.

INVITATION

I invite you to compile a list of people in your life who have been like the Good Samaritan. Using an actual pen/pencil and sheet of paper, write to someone on your list or someone else you might think of who would enjoy receiving a letter from you. Write about a time when you felt their encouragement and support. Let them know just how vital their kindness was.

Make sure you are in a safe space and then take a deep breath.

When experiencing anxiety or a depressive episode, it is difficult to not only be "in the moment," but also to feel hopeful. One way of being in the moment is to write a letter to someone.

This simple, yet profound, act of writing a letter can ground you in the present. You may feel you have accomplished something, and in the act of appreciation of another, you might even feel a glimmer of hope.

REFLECTION

- Pick one of the names from your list and write about how they reached out to you in your time of need.
- Do they know that you feel this way about them? If the person is living, how might you be able to let them know? How might you honor their memory if they are no longer with you?
- Have you ever been someone else's Good Samaritan? How did it make you feel?

SUPPLICATION

Christ, be with me. Rescue me. Christ, be with me.
The ocean's surface is rough.
The boat is sinking.
I am hoarse from crying out.
Now a silent cry for help.
Only the wind and you can hear me.
The wind blows by.
You remain.
You abide in me.
I abide in you.
I breathe you in.
You save me.
Christ, be with me. Rescue me. Christ, be with me.
Amen.

3. FEAR

Christ, be with me. I am afraid. Christ, be with me.

THE DAYS AND WEEKS FOLLOWING MY VISIT TO THE HOSPITAL WERE A blur. And the soul-crushing fear that wrapped around my throat and sat on my chest did not go away quickly as I had naively hoped.

Nights remained incredibly difficult. I was overwhelmed by fear. My own head didn't even feel like a safe space. Daytime was just as tricky. I didn't want to get out of bed. I wanted to disappear. Once filled with color, laughter, and joy, my world became exceptionally small and lonely. When I closed my eyes, I saw the bright colors spinning and swirling—disappearing like water down a drain.

The saddest thing for my wife was that we had been planning to host Christmas in our new home with her parents and her sister's family. Kristin had especially been looking forward to seeing her sister, our brother-in-law, and our nephews. Kristin and her sister have supported each other through rough patches throughout their lives, and I know that Kristin longed for her support.

We called them and told them not to come. I was devastated, embarrassed, and ashamed. I was achingly heartbroken for our families. My in-laws, already on the road, continued, uncertain of what they would find when they pulled into our driveway.

You might wonder why I didn't rush out to find a therapist or psychiatrist. It certainly would make sense to do that. Make a few calls, get on the schedule, and so on. The harsh reality was that every psychiatrist and therapist we contacted was booked out for months. As a result, many of them quit taking new patients.

No one could fit me in. But Kristin wouldn't give up. She spent hours on the phone talking with insurance representatives, receptionists, office managers, therapists, and psychiatrists and did so until she was able to get me an expedited appointment.

Following my visit to the hospital and meetings with specialists, I received an official diagnosis of Generalized Anxiety Disorder and Attention Deficit Hyperactivity Disorder, better known as ADHD. The psychiatrist prescribed something to help me sleep and medication to help with my anxiety and ADHD.

Navigating medication can be an arduous journey. There is no such thing as one-size-fits-all medical solution. It also takes time and patience for many to find what medication works best. I am not making any type of judgement or proclamation about the use of medication, or not, in the treatment of mental health. This is a personal decision that each individual makes, working with their medical team.

Along with my psychiatrist, I needed a therapist on my team. Well-meaning friends suggested the names of different Christian therapists.

Despite being a Christian and serving in the Episcopal Church, I did not necessarily want a Christian therapist. I wanted to feel better. To do that, I felt perhaps I needed to step out of what was familiar to me and hear from those outside of the world I traverse every day.

Like so many others in the world, I've had both positive and negative experiences with the Church. Growing up as the child of a clergyperson and living my entire life in a fishbowl opened me up to misdirected criticism and anger. I share a birthday with the Feast of St. Stephen and have always felt a kinship with him. He was stoned to death. The figurative stones thrown at me and my family came at us directly—but more often passively and underhandedly. Passive anger can hurt deeply.

My therapist and psychiatrist taught me how to love myself. They taught me about grace and forgiveness. They reminded me that I was wonderfully made. They taught me about Jesus's compassion in those one-on-one sessions. They listened to me.

Yes, I had to pay them. Even so, I believe that the care they imparted to me not only blessed me but saved me. It took six months of therapy, medications, rest, strategies, and patience before I started feeling better.

That's not to say I'm cured or ever will be. Mental illness is rarely that kind of disease. In fact, it is a part of what makes me who I am and perhaps makes you who you are. There are times I experience a leveling out and I feel more hopeful. And there will be seasons when the road is bumpier, the destination not as clear. I will work with my pit crew to keep me on track. Having a support team around you makes all the difference in the world.

I want to interject here and acknowledge the privilege that I have in being able to have access to such great care. Unfortunately, not everyone is so lucky and, truthfully, I carry significant guilt about that fact of the modern world.

At the same time, I feel deep gratitude and the call to use what I have learned about my health—especially my mental health—with others who have similar struggles. If transparency about my mental illness journey helps even one person, then I know that I am on the right path.

I made the decision early on that I would not be ashamed of my diagnosis. There is nothing to be ashamed of. I am open and honest. I've shared my story one-on-one, at a conference in front of 450 people, and with thousands across social media. I chose to live out loud because so many of us struggle in the shadows. If each of us share but a flicker of light with another, we will find that we are not alone.

In the years following that scary night in the emergency room, I began to understand that one of the ways I move through life has a name. I am an empath—highly sensitive to just about everything.

I feel everything. I want to make everyone happy. I try to avoid conflict. I don't know how to say no. I often care for others when I should be caring for myself. I am also very creative.

I am also moody.

Mood can be defined as a relatively stable affective state often described as positive or negative. Sometimes mood is described as one's subjective feeling state and affects the outward expression of it. Unlike emotions, which tend to be stronger and more specific, moods are more general and less intense. They are also generally not triggered by a particular experience or event. However, they can be influenced by various factors, including fatigue, stress, social interactions, world events, hormones, weather, hunger, and general health.[1]

One of the ways I have found to improve—or shift my moods—is by doing something creative.

I'm a photographer. I draw, paint, and know how to throw pottery on a wheel. In addition, I write poetry, children's picture books, and books for adults. I always have a creative project in process.

It has taken me a lifetime to come to the realization, but I now know that I am not broken but something to celebrate.

A Japanese legend tells the story of a mighty shogun warrior who broke his favorite tea bowl and sent it away for repairs. When he received it back, the bowl was held together by unsightly metal staples. Although he could still use it, the shogun was disappointed. Still hoping to restore his beloved bowl to its former beauty, he asked a craftsman to find a more elegant solution.

The craftsman wanted to try a new technique, something that would add to the beauty of the bowl as well as repair it. So, he mended every crack in the bowl with a lacquer resin mixed with gold. When the tea bowl was returned to the shogun, there were streaks of gold running through it, telling its story, and—the warrior thought—adding to its value and beauty. This method of repair became known as *kintsugi*.

Kintsugi, which roughly translates to "golden joinery," is the Japanese philosophy that the value of an object is not in its beauty, but in its imperfections, and that these imperfections are something to celebrate, not hide.[2]

One of the most important things I have learned on this journey has been the importance of engaging with that which I fear. So often, we avoid what we are most afraid of. Instead, facing these fears might be the best thing we can do to find peace. For me, this has taken the form of confronting the hurt that has impacted my life, whether by institutions or individuals.

It is said that "hurt people hurt people."

Still, those kinds of confrontations must be handled with care. The saying "hurt people hurt people" is true, but this does not make it acceptable for you to perpetuate the cycle by taking certain frustrations out on those you love the most.

Seeing an experience in its totality, both good and bad, can help to free you. While I can acknowledge that not all my experiences with the Church have been positive, I can also remember the ways the Church has carried me.

The good news? It's never too late to confront what you fear or what has affected you.

––––––––––

The winds began to blow and the boat began to toss and shudder.

"Maybe the storm will settle down," the disciples discussed among themselves.

But it did not settle down. The winds continued to strengthen, and the destructive power of the angry wind was so relentless the boat began to take on water. Jesus was weary and had fallen asleep. Even as the storm raged around him, he slept. The disciples, with great fear and anguish, awoke him.

"Lord, save us! We are perishing!"

As the winds continued to batter the failing boat, Jesus turned to them and asked a question.

"Why?"

"Why are you so afraid?"

"You of little faith."

Jesus then admonished the wind and waves, demanding their stillness. Then there was calm. And amazement.

"What sort of man is this, that even the winds and sea obey him?"

The storms continue to rage around us. Turn the TV on. Read the headlines.

"Breaking news" flashes across our screens.

Breaking news is just that—crushing, frightening, and infuriating. It breaks our collective hearts, and we are weighted down by the hopelessness.

Storms are raging all around us, and we fear the boat will sink. Political storms. Gun violence. Abuse of power. Addiction of all kinds. Violence against women. Violence against children. Violence against lesbian, gay, bisexual, and transgender people. Violence against those who worship differently or look dissimilar than we do.

"Lord, save us! We are perishing!" the disciples cried out.

"Lord, save us! We are perishing!" we cry out.

My reflection, written shortly after the tragic events of September 11, 2001, still holds true today. "When tragedy strikes, we pray that there might be survivors. Bruised and battered hands reached into the dark hoping to grasp the hand of one of the missing. We must continue to reach out away from ourselves—into the quagmire of fear and disbelief . . . into that place where there is no hope. Our hands must reach into that terrifying place where we must hang on for dear life. In that place of twisted metal and shattered dreams, we do see another hand. It reaches toward us—open, strong, forgiving, pierced. Reach out and take that hand . . . and hold on . . . for dear life."[3]

INVITATION

I invite you to reflect on something that scares you.

Personally, I am fearful of letting others down—of disappointing those I love. I'm on a journey to find out why, but for some reason, this is a fear. Of course, my mind knows that I will never be able to please everyone. My heart just hasn't caught up.

I also have medical anxiety. I am a classic hypochondriac. Every lump, bump, or ache can send me spiraling into the depths of fear. This is where I have a personal rule of not looking up any medical issue online. Mine relates to fear of illness. Yours might be fear of failure, social phobia, fear of flying, fear of heights, or fear of tight spaces.

Make sure you are in a safe space. Take a deep breath. Pray the prayer found at the beginning of this chapter or use other words that bring you to a calm place.

Using crayons, colored pencils, paints, markers, chalk, or oil pastels, create a visual response relating to fear in your life. It can be a drawing or painting. You can doodle or make a collage. As I mentioned earlier in the book, you may experience intense emotions while working on this project. Even if an exercise can eventually bring calm, it may initially have the effect of an "exposure."

In the long run, facing your fears with a creative output can shift the narrative and add an element of positivity to what you felt as wholly negative. Lean into those feelings.

Just remember to keep breathing.

If you need to take a break or put it away until you are in a better place, please do so.

REFLECTION

- What is something that scares you? Why do you think it brings you such fear?
- Are you willing to engage and face this fear? If yes, how might you do it? If not, why not?

SUPPLICATION

Christ, be with me. I am afraid. Christ, be with me
I recoil when awake.
The day does not feel safe.
The night does not feel safe.
My life does not feel safe.
I don't know where to begin.
Begin to feel safe.
In my shaking.

In my tears.
In my breaking.
Reach for me.
Hold my hand.
Hold my heart.
Hold me.
Ease my fear
Christ, be with me. I am afraid. Christ, be with me
Amen.

4. Hunger

Christ, be with me. In my craving, Christ, be with me.

I KNOW THAT I AM NOT ALONE WHEN I SAY THAT I HAVE A COMPLICATED relationship with food. I come from a long line of people for whom food isn't just what we eat. It is a religion.

Eating is central to how we gather as humans. Food, and the enjoyment of food, is a beautiful thing. Food is also important when you are working on your mental health. But this is not the book where I attempt to tell you how or what to eat.

The more I think about it, the more I realize that it is not food that I have a complicated relationship with. I have a complicated relationship with what it means to be hungry. Hunger is defined as having a strong desire or craving for something. There is the hunger for food, of course. It can also be a craving for love, normalcy (if there is such a thing), acceptance, recognition, financial security, success, friendship, forgiveness, justice, and so much more. Having a desire for these things is part of being human, and not something to be ashamed of.

Don't let anyone tell you otherwise.

I've always heard that a baby will not thrive, and may even die, if they are not held, nurtured, and cared for. I certainly believe this to be true.

Whether a newborn or a fifty-year-old, we crave touch, security, connection, and love—and we need this to live.

This desire for safety and love is programmed into each one of us.

In December 2022, my family welcomed Finley into our home. Finley, a Maltipoo, is such a bright spot in our lives. In May 2022, we bid farewell to Scout, our fifteen-and-a-half-year-old cockapoo, and we longed for a new friend.

When Finley joined us at twelve weeks old, she was practically a newborn baby. She needed us—not only to feed her and take her outside, but for comfort and safety. She still curls up in our lap, and occasionally tries to suckle my earlobe.

Just like Scout, Finley will know love, comfort, and safety. It is the commitment we made to her when we first brought her home.

Finley has other cravings. She loves plants and leaves. I'm always trying to redirect her. I'm afraid she will eat something poisonous. She also lives to run full speed—chasing a ball and keeping it from me. We live, and I work, on very busy streets, so a leash is imperative.

Like Finley, we all run into trouble sometimes. In moments of emptiness, we want to feel better, and we want to experience connection, so we may fill our lives with screen time, unhealthy eating habits, and countless other addictions and bad behaviors. If we don't redirect our own selves, we might find ourselves down a rabbit hole. We might lose sense of how we are using habits as a form of escape.

And the loss of control can lead to guilt and shame.

Guilt and shame are nothing but empty calories. We live in a society—a world—where both are as accessible as sugary candy and processed junk food. We fill our bodies with these emotions just as easy as we inhale Reese's Cups (my favorite) and Mountain Dew. It tastes and feels good for a time. In the long run, however, harm is being caused to our bodies, minds, and souls.

One palpable example of how this impacts my life is by being a "people pleaser." Perhaps you can relate. Many people who struggle with anxiety are consumed with ideas about how they are perceived and judge themselves based on how others see them. At times, I have lost sight of my own self-image.

At those times my entire self-worth is built around making others happy. Maybe I am a slow learner, but it has taken me fifty years, and countless hours of therapy, to realize that it is an impossibility. No matter how hard I try, I will never be able to make everyone happy. This is a hunger that can never be filled.

The freedom that comes from accepting this truth is life-giving.

I often hear people say that there is a "God-shaped" hole inside of us that we are trying to fill. I understand what they are trying to say, but I dislike the connotation.

God is already here. Now. Not something to plug a hole. God created us in God's image—so God's fingerprint will always be present. Although it feels like it at times, God will never leave us. God does not leave us, no matter what others may think of us, and the power of knowing this can free you.

INVITATION

You are invited to consider how you experience hunger, not just the hunger you feel in your belly, but in other parts of your life.

When you take a seat in your favorite restaurant, you are given a menu, a drink, and the waitstaff invites you to take your time on selecting what meal you would like. Or, if you are like me, you don't even need to look at the menu, because you get the same thing every time! I tend to go for what is familiar and often miss out on trying something new.

For this response, you are invited to create a menu—not of food and drink, but a menu of what you crave—of what you hunger for.

For the main entree, you might list things as concrete as a new car, or you may list something like a healthy marriage, a good night's sleep, or the repairing of a broken relationship. Not only should you list the menu item, but also include the ingredients and the cost associated with each item.

I encourage you to be creative. Name your restaurant. Design the menu. And maybe, you will come up with a menu item you haven't tried before.

Let's hope so.

REFLECTION

- What is it that you hunger most for in your life?
- When you have attempted to fill that hunger, were you satisfied? If yes, explain what that satisfaction felt like. If no, explore how it felt when you realized that you were still hungry.
- How does God fit into your hunger?

SUPPLICATION

Christ, be with me. In my craving, Christ, be with me.
I'm empty, achingly so.
A hunger so deep.
Longing for fullness.
Not from food.
I have plenty.
Help me recognize the fullness of my life.
Open my eyes.
Open my heart.
To love.
To serve.
To thrive.
Christ, be with me. In my craving, Christ, be with me.
Amen.

5. ANXIETY

Christ, be with me. Calm my anxious mind. Christ, be with me.

I'VE ALWAYS BEEN ENVIOUS OF THOSE WHO CAN "TURN OFF" THEIR minds—especially when it is time to go to sleep. I can't even imagine what that must feel like. My wife is one of those people. She closes her eyes, imagines entering a dark and quiet room, and before long, she is asleep.

I close my eyes. I imagine entering a dark room and . . . my mind is off and running. I worry and fret. I mentally engage in a conflict I had years earlier or, sometimes, from that very morning. I do a lot of "what ifs." I wonder if I'm good at anything or simply a fraudster. An imposter with a nice smile and good hair.

I wonder if it's too late.

For what? It could be anything.

I compare my life to the lives of others. I worry about death. I worry about finances. I worry about worrying. By the time I finally fall asleep, I have worried myself into exhaustion. The cycle is brutal. The only thing it accomplishes is keeping me exhausted and anxious.

And please, don't quote Matthew 6:25–34 to me:

25 "Therefore I tell you, do not worry about your life, what you will eat or what you will drink, or about your body, what you will wear. Is not life more than food, and the body more than clothing? 26 Look at the birds of the air; they neither sow nor reap nor gather into barns, and yet your heavenly Father feeds them. Are you not of more value than

they? 27 And can any of you by worrying add a single hour to your span of life? 28 And why do you worry about clothing? Consider the lilies of the field, how they grow; they neither toil nor spin, 29 yet I tell you, even Solomon in all his glory was not clothed like one of these. 30 But if God so clothes the grass of the field, which is alive today and tomorrow is thrown into the oven, will he not much more clothe you—you of little faith? 31 Therefore do not worry, saying, 'What will we eat?' or 'What will we drink?' or 'What will we wear?' 32 For it is the Gentiles who strive for all these things; and indeed, your heavenly Father knows that you need all these things. 33 But strive first for the kingdom of God and his righteousness, and all these things will be given to you as well.

34 "So do not worry about tomorrow, for tomorrow will bring worries of its own. Today's trouble is enough for today.

The birds may not worry about what to eat, and the flowers may not worry about what they wear, but I sure do. I worry about those things and so much more.

I love the above reading, but not when I probably most need to hear it.

Maybe this is the lesson. When someone is experiencing deep anxiety and worry, make space for them, pray for them, and love them. Don't quote Bible verses to them. I promise you; it is not what they need. And if you are the one experiencing the anxiety? Please don't feel bad if you don't turn to the Bible for solace in a time of angst. That might come later—or not.

Don't get me wrong—the Bible is an incredible resource to go to for comfort and healing, especially for worriers. At the same time, how some were taught to use the Bible, or seeing how others use the Bible to judge and condemn, can be a main source of anxiety. If it is this for you, you can return to it when you are ready.

In October of 2017, I drove over one thousand miles round trip, and I did it in less than four days. I had won an award from the Warren Wilson College alumni association, and I wanted to receive it in person. So, I made a weekend of it.

To earn a degree and use the student experience as a foundation to create a meaningful life is the objective for the college's graduates. At an October 7 reception during Homecoming 2017, the college recognized five different individuals, and I was honored to have been chosen as one of those selected.

The Distinguished Community Service Award is granted to an alum for distinguished accomplishment in any field of community service that brings honor to the recipient. The person's contribution may have religious, social, or educational value. The winners are people who achieve recognition among colleagues for accomplishments and service to a community.[1]

I served as a former resident assistant and member of the Chapel Crew and worked with Big Brothers Big Sisters of America and Grace Episcopal Church for my college's community engagement requirement. One of the reasons I received this honor was for my work with helping families impacted by the floods related to Hurricane Harvey. With lots of help, of course, I led a post-hurricane day camp at Palmer Church in Houston. More than twenty-five volunteers cared for upward of fifty children each day during the week that followed the flooding.

I love a road trip. And one of the stops along the way was in Oxford, Mississippi, where I attended Oxford High School. I wanted to surprise Mr. Shelby, the art teacher who took me under his wing during some incredibly turbulent times in my life. I reached out to him years earlier by phone but had not seen him in person since high school. I was so excited to tell him about my award, my family, and how he inspired me to be an artist and writer.

I pulled into Oxford and googled his address. And the first thing that popped up was his obituary. I was devastated, to say the least. In that instance, I noticed a change in my spirit. Not a good one. I began having a pain in my side. It was a deep and throbbing pain. Sometimes I would forget about it, and other times I could barely stand up. I received the award, made it through Homecoming weekend with a smile, but I was not OK.

I told Kristin about it when I got home. We scheduled an appointment with my general practitioner. He diagnosed it as a stomach virus, but the pain didn't go away.

I went to another doctor, who told me that it was probably a kidney stone. Still, no tests were done to confirm her diagnosis and the pain remained.

Not a kidney stone. Not a stomach virus. Not a pulled muscle. Not gas. So, I consulted with WebMD and diagnosed myself.

What a mistake that was.

You may remember my earlier comments about knowing I had colon cancer. Through my "research," I concluded that I was going to die much earlier than I wanted to. I started making plans. I researched how to start a GoFundMe account for my family because I was going to be leaving them with debt, loss of income, and more. And I stopped eating.

I simply wasn't hungry. I lost weight. People would tell me how good I looked. "Are you losing weight?" I would nod. "You look amazing." I wanted to tell them I was dying but decided to hold that card close to the vest.

An MRI was needed to convince me I did not have cancer. The thoughts had become so real that I searched for proof of their illegitimacy. In the searching, I was keeping the cycle going.

I share this story with you because I know that many of you have gone down the same rabbit hole and you are afraid. Every lump, bump, and pain sends you spiraling. The connection between the body and mind is incredible—holy, even. The pain I was feeling was real. You can't tell me otherwise. But I now know that it wasn't cancer, a stomach virus, or a kidney stone. It was anxiety that manifested itself as physical pain. The brain and stomach are the places where anxiety abides. I must have put out the welcome mat early on.

So, what can we do to climb off this frightening ride? To fight back? To take back the reins? We breathe and work our way back into the present moment.

We rest.

Forming new pathways in the brain takes hard work.

We eat.

Any change requires energy.

Positive change demands consistency and determination. And a healthy diet.

Watch out for those empty calories I told you about earlier.

We strive for patience.

These changes are going to take time.

We open ourselves to failure. We learn from failure. We reach for the hand of another. We move our bodies. We attend to our relationships. We find and nurture community. We accept and honor our humanity. And we set aside space for worrying. Then, when it's time to move on to something more helpful, like sleeping, we tell worry to hit the road.

The dark and quiet room practice is still a mystery to me, but I am sleeping better these days. I also haven't stopped worrying. But I've removed the welcome mat, and I've let it know that it is no longer in charge.

I am.

INVITATION

You are invited to explore what it means to rest—especially your mind.

I shared my experience of how worry impacts the quality of my sleep. You might explore the ways worry impacts your life. I have discovered that the easiest way to break the spiral of worry I so often encounter is to relocate my physical body. An example for me is when I am in bed and I am worrying about sleep, I will get up and read for a little while or go downstairs and sit in the darkness of our den until I feel sleepy.

Try to avoid finding solace in social media. That certainly doesn't help me as I descend into the web of its unhealthy distraction.

I invite you, especially if you are ruminating about something that worries you, to go for a walk. Not in the middle of the night, of course, but maybe after dinner or early in the morning.

You may not like to sweat, but I have found that when I do something that causes me to break a sweat, my worry dissipates.

When I go for a walk, I will take a mental note of the sounds around me. Maybe it is the rhythm my feet make on the pavement. The hum of traffic or the song of a bird. If there is an unfamiliar sound, I imagine that the trees are speaking to me in prose—a forest of poets. And the animals are welcoming me into their secret lives. I've come up with some crazy things. And before I know it, the thing I am worrying about is no longer as scary. Sometimes it goes away completely.

I have become more grounded—literally, my feet are on the ground—and I am moving, sweating, and breathing—breathing in the breath of the loving one who gives us breath.

There are other ways of resetting during these moments of anxiety.

- Record your thoughts into a journal. No editing. Just write.
- Light a candle—particularly one that has a fragrance that instills a spirit of calm. I am allergic to strong fragrances, so I prefer unscented. Even so, the simple act of lighting a candle can bring peace to an anxious moment.
- Another biggie for me is turning off the news. Watching too much news can cause undue stress and anxiety.

REFLECTION

- At this very moment, what are you worried about the most? Write it down—and as detailed as possible, explain why it worries you so much.
- What are your strategies for easing that worry? It might be a nap. It might be online shopping. It might be exercise. It might be alcohol. It might be eating. You might not have a strategy, and that is why you are here. Whatever it is, know that this is a safe space, without judgment, for you to consider the strategy and create others that might work better.

SUPPLICATION

Christ, be with me. Calm my anxious mind.
Christ, be with me.
My vision blurs.
My arms burn.
I want to run away.

Am I crazy?

Am I broken?

Am I going to die?

I feel like it.

I can breathe.

I can't breathe.

My head hurts.

My stomach hurts.

I want help!

I don't want help!

I'm panicking!

I'm losing it!

I need relief!

Christ, be with me. Calm my anxious mind.

Christ, be with me.

Amen.

6. STRETCH

Christ, be with me. Stretch me. Christ, be with me.

WITH THE DAWN OF EACH DAY COMES A NEW CHANCE TO SHIFT GEARS. It took me about six months of intensive therapy, medication, and the institution of various grounding practices and exercises before life regained a bit of color. One of my greatest accomplishments was waking up each morning, getting out of the bed, and taking a shower. It wasn't easy, but I knew I had to do it.

Out of everything that you are learning about me from this book, this next bit I am going to share with you might be the most embarrassing.

For people with anxiety or depression, getting out of the bed in the morning can be one of the most difficult things to do. It is also one of the most important. I would stay in bed for days—only getting up to go to the bathroom or to try to eat something, not for myself but for Kristin.

I say "for Kristin" because she is fierce and protective like a mockingbird. She would try to get me to eat—anything. We tried protein shakes (ugh) and instant grits (which I love . . . don't judge). She even made "Charlie Browns," my favorite cookie. She knew I was in trouble when I wouldn't eat those.

Your tradition may have a different name for it, but Charlie Browns are an integral part of my origin story. My Mammaw made them. My mom makes them. Now Kristin makes them. (You can find the recipe in the back of this book.)

As I mentioned before, getting out of bed at times was near impossible for me. I just wanted to hide in the dark. I wanted to be alone. I wanted to disappear. I wanted to be small like a whisper. A friend suggested that I might find some inspiration on YouTube. Maybe a gentle video with morning affirmations and encouragement.

I tried that, but it wasn't particularly helpful. It wasn't the right time for me to hear the messages.

Then, the Holy Spirit had had enough with my disinterest and self-loathing, and She intervened. At least that is what I believe happened. Somehow (the Holy Spirit), I ended up on a YouTube channel that taught yoga for pregnant women.

Yes. You read that correctly: I began practicing yoga for pregnant women.

I learned that gentle yoga and various bed exercises can help you stay in shape, both physically and emotionally, especially if you're put on bed rest during pregnancy. Through a series of stretches, breathing exercises, and the activation of muscles, I began moving my body.

The weakness and depression I had been feeling made way for the occasional giggle, and my trips out of the bed increased in frequency. Indeed, I found that adding gentle stretching and focused breathing to each day was holy medicine for my mind, body, and soul.

I found inspiration. I found humor.

I found hope.

INVITATION

Do you have a favorite recipe?

Making Charlie Browns is one of my mom's love languages. When we visit, she will almost always make Charlie Browns for us. It is love in the shape of an ugly, but oh so good, cookie.

It is safe and familiar.

For this activity, I encourage you to find a special recipe that has been passed down through your family and try your hand at making it. If you don't have a touchstone recipe like this, I encourage you to try a new recipe and create something delicious. And, if it doesn't turn out right the first time, try again! I also encourage you to enjoy what you make and to share it with someone else.

I have a friend who loves to make bread and share it with others. Cooking is her love language.

REFLECTION

• How did this activity stretch you?
• Why did you choose this recipe?

SUPPLICATION

Christ, be with me. Stretch me. Christ, be with me.
I'm comfortable.
I'm uncomfortable.
Push me.
Pull me.
Challenge and encourage me.
Change is hard.
I don't want to change.
I want everything to change.
Muscles need stretching.
I need stretching.
Before I atrophy.
Christ, be with me. Stretch me. Christ, be with me.
Amen.

7. REMEMBER

Christ, be with me in my remembering. Christ, be with me.

MEMORY IS ENRICHING AND ALSO FICKLE.

There are instances from my childhood where I remember the smells, sounds, and almost exactly how I felt in the moment. I was safe, loved, and worthy. And there are large sections of time—years—where I can't remember anything. Remembering is challenging work. And remembering, as hard as it can be, is work we must do.

I did not set out to write a book that teaches you how to stop being anxious, stop feeling things, or gain a six-pack. I wrote it because I now know I am not alone on this journey. I want you to know that you are also not alone on this journey and that there are simple ways that you can practice the art of calm. I learned a few things. I paid attention to what helped. And I want to share what I've learned.

We are human.

We feel things. We succeed.

More often, we fail.

We remember things.

Good things. Safe things.

And we, knowingly and unknowingly, pack the difficult memories away and stack them on a shelf—hidden, dusty, and forgotten.

When we engage with our memories—ESPECIALLY the hard ones—we will struggle. Looking into that box—sometimes hidden for a lifetime—may break us open again. Therefore, it is crucial to have a support system around you. Be open with your loved ones (you'll undoubtedly have to be selective) and with your most trusted friends. Let them know you are doing this work and need them to be there. Not to fix anything, but to hold space for you, your fears and tears, your anger and hurt. For whatever comes to the surface.

Obtaining the services and support of a therapist is also incredibly important. It is critical to have someone with professional skills to help you navigate the remembering. Thanks to mental health parity, more people have access to mental health professionals than in the past, but barriers remain. These days, those barriers seem to even be growing.

Shame and cost prevent many from seeking professional help. For some people, needing mental health treatment and not being able to pay for it is doubly shameful. So, they never seek the care they need. Most directly impacted by this injustice are minorities, LGBTQi+, women, and those experiencing housing or job instability.

If you have questions about health insurance and mental health services, you can find immediate help at https://www.mentalhealth.gov/get-help/health-insurance.

———————

They found my Mammaw on the floor in her kitchen. When she didn't show up for church that morning, they knew something was wrong. She had taken a pan of corn bread out of the oven and set it on the stove to cool. The smell of the sweet bread filled the kitchen. She walked down to the mailbox and returned to the kitchen, where she began to open her mail.

They found her the next day. It was a stroke, immediate and massive. I was summoned to come and see her in the hospital. It was a long drive from North Carolina to the little hospital in Louisiana. Her grandchildren gathered around her; we held her hand and told her how much we loved her.

The stroke had changed her face and rendered her unable to speak, but her eyes still sparkled, and I knew she knew I was there.

She wanted to go home to die. I was at her home when the ambulance arrived. It was a beautiful day. The birds were singing, the yellow bells in her garden were in full bloom, and her home was filled with those who loved her most. She was moved to her bedroom where she could see her beloved Louisiana sky; she was covered with one of her own homemade quilts.

Within a few short days, she was gone—finally with her Creator. Her entire life had been focused on being with the one who gave her breath. She was now really home. She was and will always be an important part of my life.

Her kitchen table became my painting table. Her handmade quilts still cover and comfort us as we fall asleep each night. Memories of our fishing trips bring me such laughter and joy.

My Mammaw's greatest gift to me was teaching me how to love, in the truest sense of the word.[1]

I share this story with you as an example of how I took a traumatic and grief-filled story from my life and entered into the act of remembering. I can now see the power and impact of my loved one's life on my life—not just on the tragic and frightening moments surrounding her death. For example, when I think about the voice of God, I hear my Mammaw's voice. My grandfather had hearing difficulty, and she would read Bible stories to him every night. I would lie in the hallway, my body halfway in the bedroom and halfway out, and listen to the stories of our faith as they came alive through her voice. Even now, I can hear her voice and it makes me smile.

This is an exercise in remembering—one I invite you to enter into.

As I have gotten older, I have become more afraid of heights. My brain often reminds me of this fear.

In 2002, I decided to climb a tree. And not just any tree. In our backyard, we have a live oak with scarred bark and outstretched branches that tell stories of childhood and hurricanes. Its roots, like memories and longing, are deep and widespread. I decided that it would be a good climbing tree. Much to my wife's dismay, and my daughter's amusement, I leaned the ladder against the tree and made my way up the trunk. Finally, I found a large branch that I prayed would hold the weight of me and my fears.

I was scared to death. I also think I short-circuited my brain. I didn't listen to what it was telling me. As I sat there, gazing across the rooftops and down at my family, I remembered climbing a similar tree in my grandparent's backyard. I remembered the feeling of the bark—the dancing shadows of the leaves. I remembered looking down at the grandparents I loved—now existing only in my memories.

Disclaimer: I'm not telling you to climb a tree, which can be a dangerous activity. I am telling you that the work of remembering is work well worth doing.

Don't go at it alone; make sure someone is holding the ladder.

INVITATION

I invite you to enter the sacred act of remembering, which can be life-giving and challenging. You want to make sure you are in a safe space. Take a deep breath. Pray the prayer at the beginning of this section or use other words that bring you to a calm place. You may also want to do this work with a therapist or trusted friend.

I shared my story of climbing a tree. I want you to try and do something you have been afraid of doing. It doesn't have to be significant; starting with something small might be the best place to begin.

Maybe you are afraid of swimming.

Take swimming lessons.

Maybe you've been afraid to return to a worshiping community because of a painful experience.

Attend worship one Sunday—invite a friend to go with you.

Maybe you need to apologize for something.

Now might be the time.

REFLECTION

- What is your earliest memory? Is this memory a good one, or a challenging or traumatic one? Explore this in your response.
- How have you engaged or overcome one or more of your fears?
- Who holds your ladder?

SUPPLICATION

Christ, be with me in my remembering.
Christ, be with me.
How have I forgotten how to play?
How have I lost my wonder?
How have I misplaced my imagination?
I can't find it.
I know it is there, but I keep coming up empty.
I am empty.
Fill me.
Fill me.
Fill me.
Help me to remember.
I am never alone.
Christ, be with me in my remembering.
Christ, be with me.
Amen.

8. MARKED

Christ, be with me. I am marked as yours forever. Christ, be with me.

MANY OF US HAVE A COMPLICATED RELATIONSHIP WITH OUR BODIES. You may have gathered that I always have. Even now, I get in the shower and look at myself—observing what I admire (not much) and what embarrasses me. I grew up in a world where men did not talk about their bodies unless they had a visible six-pack and big muscles. I have both, even if they are hiding. I also kept a list of what I despised about my body—things like my big belly, larger thighs and rear end, and big nose. I was aware of what the world recognizes as handsome. I did not see my body or face on any of those lists. Most of all, I hated taking my shirt off. I still do. Even now. I have an incredible farmer's tan that I will not show you.

My wife, Kristin, knows well that I struggle with this and, as she is wont to do, had an idea. She suggested that I get a tattoo of something that inspires me. A mark I would see each day and remember. Something that would remind me that I was more than my anxiety.

While it was a good suggestion, there was also a major problem: in the dumpster fire of my mind, I was not cool enough to have a tattoo. Only rebels and extraordinary people have tattoos.

I have a tape inside my head that says things like this. Over and over.

Lies.

Many of us have a running dialogue that works against us. Manifestations of some kind of fear or feeling of inadequacy.

That's all they are.

I told her I would think about it.

What would I choose to put on my body that would be there for the rest of my life? I spent countless hours searching, imagining, and envisioning what my tattoo would be.

I decided on a bluebird.

"The bluebird is a symbol of hope, love, and renewal and is also a part of many Native American legends. It symbolizes the essence of life and beauty. Dreaming of bluebirds often represents happiness, joy, fulfillment, hope, prosperity, and good luck."[1]

Hope. Love. Renewal. Happiness. Joy. Fulfillment. Prosperity. Good luck.

I wanted to work with a skilled artist, so I received my tattoo after being on a six-month waitlist. It was an unreal experience. I was emotional, excited, and scared. The pain was immense, but strangely, the pain was energizing.

It is not uncommon to experience feelings of euphoria while getting inked. I learned (and experienced) that when getting a tattoo, your body releases endorphins. Endorphins are naturally occurring chemicals that are produced by your body to relieve stress and pain. When released, they cause a euphoric feeling.

I still struggle with my body. I am also much more grateful for it now. I see its power, and I recognize its limitations. And I see a bluebird.

I see hope. I see renewal. I see resurrection.

I'd be remiss if I didn't mention in this chapter my love of baptism—in particular, the baptism liturgy in the Episcopal Church. The act of "marking" is experienced both verbally and in the actual physical act of marking.

Thanksgiving Over the Water

The Celebrant blesses the water, first saying

Celebrant:	The Lord be with you.
People:	And with your spirit.
Celebrant:	Lift up your hearts.
People:	We lift them up to the Lord.
Celebrant:	Let us give thanks to the Lord our God.
People:	It is right to give him thanks and praise.

Celebrant

We thank you, Almighty God, for the gift of water. Over it the Holy Spirit moved in the beginning of creation. Through it you led the children of Israel out of their bondage in Egypt into the land of promise. In it your Son Jesus received the baptism of John and was anointed by the Holy Spirit as the Messiah, the Christ, to lead us, through his death and resurrection, from the bondage of sin into everlasting life.

We thank you, Father, for the water of Baptism. In it we are buried with Christ in his death. By it we share in his resurrection. Through it we are reborn by the Holy Spirit. Therefore in joyful obedience to your Son, we bring into his fellowship those who come to him in faith, baptizing them in the Name of the Father, and of the Son, and of the Holy Spirit.

At the following words, the Celebrant touches the water

Now sanctify this water, we pray you, by the power of your Holy Spirit, that those who here are cleansed from sin and born again may continue for ever in the risen life of Jesus Christ our Savior.

To him, to you, and to the Holy Spirit, be all honor and glory, now and for ever. *Amen.*

Consecration of the Chrism

The Bishop may then consecrate oil of Chrism, placing a hand on the vessel of oil, and saying

Eternal Father, whose blessed Son was anointed by the Holy Spirit to be the Savior and servant of all, we pray you to consecrate this oil, that those who are sealed with it may share in the royal priesthood of Jesus Christ; who lives and reigns with you and the Holy Spirit, for ever and ever. Amen.

The Baptism

Each candidate is presented by name to the Celebrant, or to an assisting priest or deacon, who then immerses, or pours water upon, the candidate, saying

N., I baptize you in the Name of the Father, and of the Son, and of the Holy Spirit. *Amen.*

When this action has been completed for all candidates, the Bishop or Priest, at a place in full sight of the congregation, prays over them, saying

Let us pray.

Heavenly Father, we thank you that by water and the Holy Spirit you have bestowed upon *these* your servants the forgiveness of sin, and have raised *them* to the new life of grace. Sustain *them*, O Lord, in your Holy Spirit. Give *them* an inquiring and discerning heart, the courage to will and to persevere, a spirit to know and to love you, and the gift of joy and wonder in all your works. *Amen.*

Then the Bishop or Priest places a hand on the person's head, Marking on the forehead the sign of the cross [using Chrism if desired] and

N., you are sealed by the Holy Spirit in Baptism and marked as Christ's own for ever. *Amen.*

How beautiful are the words "marked as Christ's own forever."

I once served at a church that went through a significant restoration process. The project quickly went from a $2,000,000 project into an $8,000,000 project.

> Over two hundred years, the well-known South Carolina historic landmark had deteriorated from use and deferred maintenance, as well as many problems associated with age—cracking stucco, leaking spires and louvers, water damage, electrical challenges, heating and air-conditioning retrofit needs, stained-glass-window repair, as well as significant structural challenges. Experts carefully restored technically difficult structural components, along with wood ceilings, walls, stained glass, spires, system retrofits, etc., while craftsmen carefully refurbished other historic millwork and pews by hand, in a temporary carpenter workshop established on-site.[2]

When the time came to restore the church pews, it was discovered that the pews where the acolytes sit—where they've sat for two hundred years—were covered with marks, scratches, initials, and more carved into the wood. There were those who wanted the marks to be removed, sanded away, and painted over. And there were those who felt that these young people across the ages were attempting to *make their mark*—and these marks needed to remain. I honestly don't remember who won out. But it was an eye-opening conversation.

INVITATION

It's time to put this book down, get on your walking shoes, and, if the weather allows, go for a stroll around your neighborhood. If the weather isn't conducive to being outside, find a place indoors. Suppose you have physical challenges or limitations that prevent you from walking. In that case, I encourage you to drive with a friend or explore the neighborhood from your wheelchair or other mobility devices. Give this activity twenty or so minutes.

Although it will be good exercise for the body, I am more interested in exercising your brain. Note all the logos, symbols, watermarks, and tattoos you see. I also encourage you to pay attention to the sidewalk's surface, light posts, and walls. And graffiti! I love graffiti. You might see something scratched into the sidewalk like "R + K = 4-EVER!"

This etching on the sidewalk is like a watermark. As a photographer, I have learned the importance of including a watermark when you share your work—especially across social media. A logo, text, or signature superimposed onto a photograph is a watermark. Watermarks are typically transparent, so those viewing the image can admire it while also knowing where it came from.

I'm not encouraging you to paint on walls! Instead, I want you to note how these artists are "making their mark." Graffiti artists often get a bad rap, but I find their work healing and informative.

Graffiti that speaks to injustice and oppression is particularly moving.

I invite you to design your watermark, tattoo design, or logo that honors your life, your journey, and your story.

You can create this image with various art supplies, or use an online program like Canva or ProCreate.

REFLECTION

- How does your relationship with your body impact you?
- What is one way you can begin to honor and celebrate your body?
- Describe your watermark.

SUPPLICATION

Christ, be with me. I am marked as yours forever.
Christ, be with me.
You are.
I am.
Creator.
Artist.
Composer.
Sculptor.
Baker.
Dancer.
Singer.
Healer.
Lover.
Your fingerprint remains.
On my forehead.
On my tongue.
In my heart.

In my rest.

In my work.

Cocreators.

Marked by the holy.

Marked as holy.

Christ, be with me. I am marked as yours forever.

Christ, be with me.

Amen.

9. Anger

Christ, be with me in my anger. Christ, be with me.

In my book *My Favorite Color Is Blue. Sometimes.*, I use color to help the reader navigate feelings of grief. I chose red for love. I also chose red for anger. That's because love and anger are sisters. They share secrets and so much more.

One of my favorite stories from the Bible is where Jesus enters the Temple and loses it. Tables begin to fly. Veins bulge. Spit flies. Jesus was pissed. It's a very different picture of the Jesus we so often see. Handsome Jesus. Smiling Jesus. A twinkle in his eye. He welcomes the children. He invites the stranger. I love that Jesus.

I've also come to love angry Jesus.

I feel a connection to his anger.

I feel a connection to his weariness.

I feel a connection to his frustration.

Author and New Testament lecturer Stephen Voorwinde writes, "Although often sourced in his foreknowledge, the way Jesus handles his anger provides a model for Christians today. He knows how to be indignant, irate, and even furious, but without the slightest trace of derision, contempt, or abuse."[1]

In engaging with my own relationship with anger, I've realized that I move through life as a peacemaker and am quickly taken advantage of by others.

I navigate this life journey as an empath. I am a deep feeler. I take on the pain of others. And God forbid if someone is angry at me.

"Being an empath means you are highly sensitive, and can easily take on other people's emotions." Empaths are often considered to be emotional sponges, which understandably can be very draining. It takes empathy to an entirely different level.

Common empath traits can include being:

- extremely sensitive
- highly intuitive
- thoughtful, kind, and giving
- a great listener
- independent
- easily overwhelmed (people, noises, smells, and other stimulations)
- introverted (may appear shy or quiet)
- strongly averse to conflict[2]

Once someone I worked for invited me into their office under the guise of checking in on me, only to pelt me, behind closed doors (out of sight of others), with threats and demeaning accusations. It was unexpected and shocking. This person knew me well, saw an opening in my heart, and went for it like a rabid animal.

I still carry invisible scars from this devastating experience.

In my mind, anger was something you did to hurt someone else, and I didn't want to hurt anyone. I have come a long way. I now understand that anger—particularly righteous anger—is essential. Anger can be life-giving and lifesaving.

When I was sixteen, Tracy Chapman released the song "Fast Car." I'm sure you know it. If you don't, do yourself a favor and give it a listen. Tracy Chapman and I don't look alike. We haven't faced the same injustices. But Tracy Chapman and this song gave me the gift of understanding how to express anger.

"Fast Car" and every other song on that album express righteous anger. Her words, holy and ripe with truth, took the world by storm. Tracy harnessed her anger, recognized its power, and released it into the world. She sings about racism, poverty, sexism, governmental abuse, etc. But she found a way to channel her anger in a beautiful way, and the result changed the world. Her words are still changing the world. With the times rarely as difficult as they are now, "Fast Car" is as timely now as it was when she released the song in 1988.

When filled with anger, those around us—or those in our head—tell us that we need to calm down, that anger is wrong, that we need to get over it. I do not believe that anger is destructive. I do not believe that we need to *get over it*. I do not believe that we need to *calm down*. Sometimes the last thing I want to do is calm down.

I do believe that how we channel our anger is of utmost importance. When we bottle our emotions—especially anger—we are at significant risk for this anger to come out when we least expect it. It might come out as violence. It might come out as self-harm. It might come out as an addiction.

We would be burying our heads in the sand if we didn't recognize how, in our own country and lives, anger and how we express this anger has created what feels like a ticking time bomb.

For some, that time bomb has already gone off, and far too many innocent children and adults have paid the price.

———————

One of the many things I have learned about myself over the past few years is that I must engage with my anger. As I shared above, I did not always feel like I had permission or the power to express my anger. I allowed people to walk over me. I allowed people to ignore or disrespect me. I smiled, apologized, and apologized again.

My dad is a retired Episcopal priest. As the child of a clergy-person, I had a front-row seat from where I saw the Church at its best and worst. Recalling my parents' fortitude in the face of challenging circumstances can help soothe my spirit when anger bubbles up within. And I love that they are both now retired and enjoying so many more aspects of their lives. My mom will excitedly text me photos of the eggs their chickens are laying. My dad texts me about how proud he is of me.

When the crash I experienced after Hurricane Harvey brought me to my knees, I began to see the importance of anger—mainly as I started to long for a calm spirit in my life. One of the ways I began to express my anger was to cry. That may sound like a weak way to respond to anger, but tears are not a sign of weakness.

Let me repeat it.

Tears are not a sign of weakness.

Crying is an important safety valve, largely because keeping difficult feelings inside—what psychologists call repressive cop-ing—can be bad for our health. Studies have linked repressive coping with a less resilient immune system, cardiovascular disease, and hypertension, as well as with mental health conditions, includ-ing stress, anxiety, and depression.[3] Crying has also been shown to increase attachment behavior, encouraging closeness, empathy, and support from friends and family.[4]

I come from a crying family. There's never a lack of tears. For many, though, especially boys and men, tears are not encouraged, recognized, or allowed. And this makes me angry. As my friend Sasha told me one day while sitting in my office, "Tears represent energy that needs to be released." There is no shame in releasing anger through tears.

But you can't stop there. I began standing up for myself—in small ways at first. I questioned decisions that were made instead of just going along with them. I began to recognize how my body responded to anger, and I allowed these feelings to come out in healthier and more proactive ways. I still cry when I get angry. I still allow myself to get hurt by others. I still allow people to walk over me. And I still box up my anger when I should express it.

Now, though, I also know that my life and my voice matter. My anger matters.

While we are at it, the sixteen-year-old kid in me—and the fifty-year-old in me—longs to meet Tracy Chapman. So, I want to tell her "thank you." Thank you for teaching me to be angry. Thank you for giving voice to my anxiety and fear.

Thank you for reminding me that I am someone.

INVITATION

I invite you to practice a form of breath prayer or gratitude prayer. I use this practice in my daily life. I also use it with children I serve as a Christian educator.

Think of something you do all day, every day. You breathe, of course. If you are not breathing, that might require additional action.

Please take a deep breath, hold it, and then let it out. Repeat this three times—there is no need to rush it.

I then want you to do one of two things. First, if you are entering this as a prayer and wish to address God, I invite you to "give" God a name or role. For example, I might address God as "Creator God." As you breathe in, speak within your heart the words "Creator God" or whatever opening you choose. As you breathe out, offer a thanksgiving—"Thank you for this day." Or you can speak a personal mantra or other words you choose.

Breathe in—"Creator God"

Breathe out—"Thank you for the day."

You can repeat this for as long as you like—or in my case until I fall asleep.

REFLECTION

- How did this exercise impact your breathing?
- How did this exercise redirect or settle your anger?
- How might you use this exercise in your daily life? Where? When?

SUPPLICATION

Christ, be with me in my anger. Christ, be with me.
I am shaking.
Shake me.
I am angry.
Be angry with me.
I scream.
Scream with me.
I lash out.
Lash out with me.
I cry.
Years of pain.
Years of frustration.
Years of grief.
I am angry.
I am ANGRY.
Stand with me.
Christ, be with me in my anger. Christ, be with me.
Amen.

10. Toxic

Christ, be with me in places of toxicity. Christ, be with me.

ONE OF THE MOST CHALLENGING THINGS I HAVE EVER HAD TO DO IS recognize when a relationship needs to change significantly or end. And then address it.

Relationships end. We turn in our resignation, or we receive a pink slip. We fall out of love. Our journeys take different directions. We experience hurt, and the relationship remains damaged or broken even after acknowledging and addressing that hurt. This is especially painful when a relationship has become toxic. Toxic relationships serve no one. They only serve feelings of anxiety, grief, anger, disappointment, and resentment. A relationship undergirded by these feelings is no longer a relationship that feeds you or your soul. Instead, the foundation of these relationships will crack and sink.

No different than the foundation that failed beneath our home.

The other thing I have learned is that simply because a relationship has ended, you don't have to look at it as a failure or with disdain. I have several old relationships that I can look back on with gratitude and joy. These relationships carried me—and I carried these relationships. The memories of these relationships remain special and good.

They also have changed. I have changed.

I remember waking up one morning after a challenging season in my life—not only in my personal life but also in my professional life—and I knew I had to make a change. My presence in these relationships had become toxic, and the relationships I remember with love and gratitude had also become toxic. So, I resigned—both professionally and personally. It was time, and it was the responsible thing to do.

Resigning from an organization you've spent a lifetime with and love dearly is not easy.

Resigning from a relationship with dear friends and colleagues is especially difficult. But I did it, and you can too.

I knew that my and the organization's health depended on it. Once I made that decision, I was able to sleep better. I could move through my day with hope and joy, not anger and hurt. I made my mental, physical, and spiritual health a priority.

I grieve for these broken relationships, but the newfound space opened up possibilities for new relationships. New opportunities. Anxiety and shame were replaced with experiences that have helped me see the world much more expansively and inclusively.

———————

One summer afternoon on the dock at our local park, I experienced the realization that my friendship group has grown but also evolved into a tribe that looks nothing like the one I was a part of many years ago. Now, our common language may not be English. Instead, it is photography—particularly, nature photography.

Relationships change. Relationships end. Relationships expand. And, again, I am hopeful that some relationships might experience resurrection.

INVITATION

Reflect on the relationships in your life that you might define as toxic. Consider reaching out to someone on your list and invite them to coffee or a meal.

I work near the museum district here in Houston, and I often invite people to join me for the latest exhibit. I especially like doing this with individuals I am struggling with—or they with me. It is neutral ground—a safe and comfortable place to be. We visit with each other, explore all kinds of beauty, and, as a result of this intentionality, we are able to better understand each other and what our difficulties might be.

Be open to this exercise. Maybe you are introverted or maybe the conversation will just be slow to get going. If so, then honor the quiet moments. Speaking less and listening more is always a good path to choose.

REFLECTION

- How did this exercise challenge or encourage you?
- Reflect on different relationships in your life. How might some of these relationships exhibit toxicity?
- Is there someone famous or otherwise important to you that you would like to invite to join you? Why them?

SUPPLICATION

Christ, be with me in places of toxicity. Christ, be with me.
Where once I found strength and friendship,
I now find pain.
Judgment.
Cold shoulder.
I am not inspired.
I am anxious.
I am defensive.
This is not a healthy relationship.
Help me to recognize when it is time to let go.
Time to give thanks for what was.

Look with gratitude for what is.
Look with anticipation for what will be.
Christ, be with me in places of toxicity. Christ, be with me.
Amen.

11. FALLOW

Christ, be with me in this fallow season. Christ, be with me.

MY EARLIEST MEMORIES OF THE OUTDOORS TAKE PLACE IN THE GARden—my grandparents' garden. I spent countless spring days helping my grandparents plant tomatoes, water the green beans, pick the figs, dig potatoes, and so much more. Much of my grandparents' food came from their garden. Surrounded by green pine trees and blue Louisiana skies, I learned about planting seeds, tending to them, and watching them grow. My grandparents used almost every part of their two-acre lot for this purpose. They also had purple martin boxes. So even now, when I hear the song of a purple martin, I am carried back to my childhood.

I now know how much work went into preparing the soil for the bounty of vegetables that fed our family. I still remember what the table looked like, covered in colors of the rainbow from the garden.

In my mind's eye, I see tomatoes the color of sunset, golden-fried catfish pulled fresh from the creek earlier that same day, and I can taste the slimy green saltiness of boiled okra (my favorite!). Dessert was often a slice of warmed pound cake and berries, served on Corelle dessert plates.

When agricultural land is left fallow, the nutrients in the soil are replenished. My grandparents would tend the soil—tilling it and adding fertilizer, sand, and other mixtures into the ground. But they would not plant in it for a growing season or more.

This practice of letting land lie fallow is a practice that can be applied to our lives. One of the things I learned when I began treatment for my anxiety was that the soil from where my passion, ideas, energy, and health grow had been completely tapped out. The soil of my soul, in other words, was no longer fertile. It was dry, crumbling, and no longer bearing fruit.

I avoided conflict. I never said no. I would produce and produce and produce—never noticing just how little the nutrients remaining in the garden of my soul had become. As a farmer tends to their land, I should have been tending to my soul. But I had forgotten how and could offer up only versions of myself that were weak, brittle, and less personable. I felt flavorless, and a life without flavor is not a life at all. Without flavor and passions, growth no longer occurs.

Not until experiencing my mental health crisis had I realized the importance of tending to the soil of my soul. It wasn't until I remembered how my grandparents tended to their garden that I understood the importance of letting your soul lie fallow.

Things had to change. For me, it began with my basic needs. We need food, shelter, water, rest, and love to thrive. As I shared earlier, I wasn't sleeping very well. The foundations of my shelter were crumbling too. When it came to food, I either wouldn't eat at all or would eat in excess. For any change to occur, I had to prioritize my health by making better choices.

I had to relearn how to eat. I also had to learn how to sleep. While I eventually made progress, it certainly didn't happen overnight (pun intended). The change took time, as new habits are, by definition, formed over longer periods of time. But the journey was worth the effort. I can now quiet my mind and know how to make self-care a priority. That includes saying no to people when necessary and yes to opportunities that bring me connection and joy. While I'm far from perfect in all of these areas, the progress is what matters. It's what brings hope and light where there only used to be despair and darkness.

I have this great fear of letting people down. And what I have learned is that I am more likely to disappoint others when I am not caring for myself. One of the most significant examples of this is how I honored my creative spirit.

Along with being a writer and photographer, I am also a painter. I began painting when I entered junior high school.

One of my favorite art teachers, Mr. Gingles, introduced me to the work of Antoni Tàpies and Cy Twombly. Antoni Tàpies and Cy Twombly works were like my life—messy, scattered, telling stories with scribbles and smears. And, for a teenage boy searching for an identity, their work opened my mind and introduced me to a new language. The language of art.

When anxiety reared its ugly head in my life, I realized that it had been years since I had sat down in front of a canvas and painted something just for myself.

I have sold hundreds, if not thousands, of paintings. But unfortunately, I had become a machine and had forgotten *myself*. One way I began to tend to that soil was to recognize the healing power of making art, not for the consumption of others but for my own enjoyment. The amount of anxiety, guilt, and shame I felt when creating something simply for pleasure was immense. No longer. Now making art for the sake of creating is part of my daily ritual.

Anxiety, guilt, and shame are quite the trio. I tilled them into the soil like the fertilizer they are and watched with awe at what began to grow.

INVITATION

You are invited to spend some time at a farmer's market.

This is an exercise I would encourage you to do seasonally. For example, the bounty will look different in spring than in winter.

In the spring you might see baskets brimming with beets, carrots, tomatoes, peppers, green beans, and broccoli. You might even see farm-fresh eggs and bouquets of flowers. In the winter, you'll likely see leafy vegetables like cabbage, kale, collard greens, rutabagas, and pumpkins. You might also see canned vegetables and fall decorations made from dried flowers.

Take a camera or sketchpad with you. Take photos or draw pictures of the vegetables and gifts from the garden or farm. Notice the colors. The textures. The different aromas. If you would prefer to write than draw or take photos, try penning a poem or short story based on your visit.

I also encourage you to schedule a visit to a large vegetable garden, flower garden, or working farm. Notice the different crops and how the gardeners and farmers use the land.

How does the change of seasons impact the different crops?

REFLECTION

- What is your biggest takeaway from this activity?
- How is your health impacted by the change of seasons or transitions in your life?
- What season of life are you in now? How might you apply the idea of fallow land to your own life?

SUPPLICATION

Christ, be with me in this fallow season.
Christ, be with me.
Seasons change.
I change.
The soil of my spirit is dry.
Not fertile.
Life-giving waters have dried up.

They take and take.
I give and give.
And then there is nothing left.
I am exhausted.
I am dying.
I am nothing.
Give me rest.
Give me rest.
Give me rest.
Rest.
Your restorative love is what I need.
Christ, be with me in this fallow season.
Christ, be with me.
Amen.

12. WALK

Christ, be with me in my walking. Christ, be with me.

AT THIS POINT IN THE BOOK, I WILL LIKELY SURPRISE NO ONE BY CONfessing I've spent most of my life hating exercise. What may or may not be more revealing, however, is where that sentiment began: junior high PE class.

Hell on earth for any awkward kid. Not only did we have to change clothes in the presence of others, but we were also forced to compete against each other day after day. For someone who was already uncomfortable in their skin and felt embarrassed to show their own body, the scars left by PE class are deep ones.

Let me set the stage: PE class 1985. In the throes of puberty, the last thing I wanted to do was participate in mandatory PE class. To add to the horrific nature of this experience, you must understand that the coach was also my algebra teacher, and the hate I have for math might be as high as the hatred I have for PE class. Try not to be jealous, but I was *lucky* enough to get two doses of this man each day!

I failed an algebra test earlier that morning, so I knew "coach" had it in for me. You can imagine my horror when I learned that during PE, we were going to run a relay race. There would be two teams, and the teams would compete.

Yippie!

Another chance for me to embarrass myself and let down the team. Then came the best part: we were to run the race backward.

You can only imagine what was going through my head. I couldn't run forward, and now I was expected to run backward? Coach must have really hated me.

Then came my turn. The air in the gym was sticky, hot, and smelled like armpits and Drakkar Noir. It was smothering. Every eye was on me. I started running. Backward. I could hear the *Chariots of Fire* theme. I was going to make it!

And then, because, you know, it was me, I tripped over my own feet and started falling. A slow-motion crash scene ensued. Everyone was staring. I instinctively threw my hands back to catch myself. The act of doing this had grave consequences.

I still hit my head, but I also landed hard on my hands, straining both wrists and injuring the ligaments. I was beyond mortified. I am sure I acted tough and then cried when no one was watching.

This "car crash" could've ended there, but in typical Roger style, it didn't. I ended up having to wear splints and Ace bandages on both wrists. These splints held my wrists fixed in place—hands bent forward at the wrists.

You know how classy junior high boys can be. I was called all kinds of names. The only one I can share with you is T. rex. Horrible, right?

Fast-forward to the spring of 2020—right around the beginning of the pandemic—and I was heavier than I had been in a long time. While it took the world coming to a standstill for me to realize I had to do something with my health, the moment had finally arrived.

For me and my body, the heavier I am, the less healthy I am. My blood pressure increases, I sleep less, eat more, and generally feel miserable. I needed to make a change.

So, one day, I woke up early and decided to go for a walk. At first, I walked around the block. I'd be lying if I said I enjoyed it. Chubby legs rubbing together. Add sweat to the mix, and then Texas-sized mosquitoes.

As you can imagine, I came up with many reasons why walking was not for me. But I'm hardheaded, so I went to Target, bought some spandex shorts, added a splash of powder, and kept walking. After getting bored with just walking around the block, I decided to walk around the neighborhood lake and added a few more blocks. Before too long, I was walking six miles a day. I cannot stress enough how vital walking has become to my mental and spiritual health. Physically, my legs are stronger, my blood pressure is lower, and I am falling in love with the power of my body, maybe for the first time ever.

I tend to look back over my life with regret—and I did that with walking. Why did it take me so long to discover the pleasure walking now brings me? Why couldn't I have started this in my twenties or thirties? Maybe the answer is that I wasn't ready.

I still have a very complicated relationship with math, and I try not to think about "coach" and PE. Although I love telling the story of the time I had to walk around like a T-Rex.

INVITATION

In an earlier chapter, you were invited to go for a walk. I also want to honor and recognize those who cannot walk physically or struggle with other mobility issues. Instead of the physical act of walking, I want to invite you to take a mental journey—almost a guided meditation of sorts.

Make sure you're in a comfortable position for meditation. It doesn't matter whether you lie down or sit.

Begin by slowing your breath and closing your eyes.

Imagine a place where you're happy and calm. Think about somewhere you've been or a place you'd like to go.

As you imagine this place, I invite you to focus on your different senses. In this place that you have journeyed to, take note of what fragrances you recognize. Is it the smell of baking bread? Or maybe salt air from your favorite beach?

Envision yourself completely immersed in this setting. Pay attention to your breath. Feel your muscles relax.

What are the sounds that you hear? Are there familiar voices? Do you hear music? Or are you surrounded by silence?

In this place, you experience deep peace and calm. As it washes over you, I invite you to wiggle your fingers and toes. Open your eyes when you are ready to leave this place.

REFLECTION

- How do you make space for wonder and imagination in your life?
- Where did you journey to? Why did you choose to make this journey?
- My personal story includes a bit of personal tragedy and humor. So how does laughter impact your spirit of calm?

SUPPLICATION

Christ, be with me in my walking. Christ, be with me.
Walk with me.
In my fear.
In my joy.
In my grief.
In my anger.
In my disbelief.
In my laughter.
In my solitude.
In my noise.
In my panic.
In my rest.

In my waking.
In my walking.
Christ, be with me in my walking. Christ, be with me.
Amen.

13. SEE

Christ, be with me in my seeing. Christ, be with me.

"SYNESTHESIA IS HEARING MUSIC AND SEEING SHAPES. OR HEARING A word and seeing a color. Essentially, synesthesia is the sensation of experiencing one of your senses through another."[1]

I've often wondered if I have a subtle form of it. My earliest memories are filled with music, color, shapes, and patterns. This is where I found solace. I found safety in patterns. I found hope in color. I like to imagine that I see the world like Vincent van Gogh.

What am I in the eyes of most people—a nonentity, an eccentric, or an unpleasant person—somebody who has no position in society and will never have; in short, the lowest of the low. All right, then—even if that were absolutely true, then I should one day like to show by my work what such an eccentric, such a nobody, has in his heart. That is my ambition, based less on resentment than on love in spite of everything, based more on a feeling of serenity than on passion. Though I am often in the depths of misery, there is still calmness, pure harmony and music inside me. I see paintings or drawings in the poorest cottages, in the dirtiest corners. And my mind is driven towards these things with an irresistible momentum.[2]

I recognize how he experienced the world around him as a complicated, rich, confusing, infuriating, lonely, and intensely beautiful place. Dare I say that I also identify with his complex mind and the struggles he experienced.

When I began walking, I started seeing the world in new ways. At first, I would fill my ears with music or the latest podcast. My goal was to walk, and that was it. Maybe that is why I experienced failure in the past. I lost interest when the plan was just walking.

So, one day, I decided to walk around the neighborhood without my headphones. At first, all I noticed were the sounds of cars passing by or the occasional airplane flying overhead. I became bored with that exercise, so I decided to focus my attention no further than ten feet from where my own feet touched the ground. This meant I spent a lot of time looking at the pavement or the sidewalk. Imperceptibly at first, I began noticing textures, imprints, patterns, and more. I imagined that the sidewalk was a book, but instead of pages telling a story, it was the concrete's surface.

I was an archeologist looking for fossils. An archivist looking at memories engraved in the ground upon which I walked. Some mornings the light was bright and the shadows sharp. I took note of how the light spilled across the sidewalk's surface. Instead of looking at the weeds that grew from cracks in the sidewalk, I would see the shadow these weeds made.

Shadows helped me see the light.

I didn't realize at the time that I was experiencing groundedness. I was focused on the present and not worried about the past. I was not fretting over the what-ifs of the future. I was not afraid or lonely. I was at home in my own body. I was not simply looking; I was seeing.

There is a difference.

We do a lot of looking. Looking at screens and mirrors. Looking for love. Looking for the next best thing. I wanted to share my discovery with others. I knew I wasn't the only one moving through life without seeing everything around me.

So, I started taking photographs with my phone. Initials carved into wet cement. Imprints of leaves and love long faded. Shadows and footprints. Weeds burst forth from tiny cracks.

I began posting my photos on Facebook. At first, there was very little response or reaction. But before long, people began commenting. They expressed curiosity and interest. They wanted to know why and how. More than anything, they wanted to know if they could do it and would ask me how to get started.

I began noticing that others were taking photos on their walks. Someone would suggest a theme like flowers, patterns, or lines, and my Facebook feed would soon be filled with these incredible images. We were learning to see—together.

I even offered to lead a weekly session on Zoom where we would explore contemplative photography and "learning to see." I didn't think anyone would participate. Much to my surprise, I had to close registration at twenty participants. The incredible thing about this weekly class was that we were located all over the country. Zoom allowed us to create a community. I assigned a theme each week that included selfies, circles, light, shadows, textures, and reflections, or I would assign a color like blue. In our searching and seeing, we found each other.

We found hope through the holy sharing of our visual prayers.

It was early morning when I decided to get out of the bed and go for a walk down to the ocean.

We often say the sky is "up there," when really the sky surrounds us and is inside of us. We breathe it in, and lungs are filled. We often say Jesus is "up there," when really Jesus surrounds us and is inside of us. We breathe his breath, and our lungs are filled.

Sleep had been hard to come by that night. As it often is, my mind was full and racing. It was at a time in my life where I was facing some tough decisions both in my personal and professional life, and I thought that the fresh ocean air would help clear my head.

The salt-tinged morning air was filled with the sounds of excited seagulls—like children on a playground. Blurs of white and gray, darting this way and that, telling stories that grow more fantastical with each splash of the waves. I continued to soak in the beauty of the early morning light. I gazed out across the expanse of the ocean and set my eyes toward the horizon—that illusory yet intriguing place where the sky seems like it's meeting the earth.

As a child, I would often draw a thin line of sky at the top of the paper—and a round sun in the upper corner. I was thinking of those illustrations when some unusual movement down the beach caught my attention. It was a small tree, maybe six feet tall, and it looked like it was on fire. I saw flashes of orange and yellow and it was engulfed in what I thought were flames.

I ran down the boardwalk toward the burning tree. Then I stopped, frozen in my tracks. The tree was not on fire. It was engulfed, though, with hundreds, maybe thousands, of monarch butterflies, their wings dancing to the ancient rhythm of creation.

I stood there and wept with joy. I felt like I was the horizon, where the sky came down and touched the earth.

There are these two young fish swimming along, and they happen to meet an older fish swimming the other way, who nods at them and says, "Morning, boys, how's the water?" And the two young fish swim on for a bit, and then eventually one of them looks over at the other and goes, "What the hell is water?"[3]

There are moments in our lives; there are moments in a day when we seem to see beyond the usual. Such are the moments of our greatest happiness. Such are the moments of the greatest wisdom. If one could but recall this vision by some sort of sign. It was in this hope that the arts were invented. Signposts on the way to what may be. Signposts toward greater knowledge.[4]

Why do the flames that flicker on candles catch our eye?

Why do we stop at the edge of the ocean—eyes focused on the blue—spirit soaring in the mist of crashing waves?

Why does a certain song transport us to another time—another place?

Why does a painting, a sculpture, a photograph, or a simple sketch give us pause?

In these times of awareness we can see the exceptional—the holy. We sense God's presence in our lives. We experience God's presence in the colors and sounds that surround us. It is the catch in your breath—the chills down your spine.

INVITATION

You are invited to participate in a special art activity. For those of you who have taken drawing classes, you may have already done this. I find it equally frustrating and so much fun.

You will enjoy it if you allow yourself to do so. (Profound words, right?)

You can do this in a couple of different ways.

Create a still life of found objects—you will then draw this still life. The catch is that you will not look at your drawing or the pencil while doing this exercise. Instead, look only at the still life—try to be open enough that your eyes communicate directly with the pencil.

The other way to do this is to have someone sit for you so you can draw their portrait. Keep your pencil on the paper and draw their likeness with one line—never lifting the pencil off the paper. Again, let your eyes communicate directly with the pencil.

Draw what you see—not what you think you see.

This activity can be lots of fun—and who knows, you might just come up with something you really like!

REFLECTION

- What did it feel like to draw without looking at your drawing? How did you feel when you finished?
- What are other ways you can explore the idea of seeing vs. looking?

SUPPLICATION

Christ, be with me in my seeing. Christ, be with me.
I look but fail to see.
Open my eyes.
Open my heart.
Open my hands.
Take mud from the earth.
Spit from your mouth.
Put it on my eyes.
I want to see.
I long to see your face.
In the faces of my loved ones.
In the faces of my enemies.
I look, but I do not see.
Christ, be with me in my seeing. Christ, be with me.
Amen.

14. LISTEN

Christ, be with me—help me to hear. Christ, be with me.

AS I WRITE THIS, I AM TAKING NOTE OF JUST HOW QUIET OUR HOME is. I've taken the day off to work. I spent the morning in the woods on a trail, listening for birds. Now I am home writing to you.

In the previous chapter, I shared some about what it means to look and what it means to see. I will do a bit of the same thing with this chapter, only this time with listening and hearing.

As someone who experiences mild to moderate hearing loss, I know just how precious hearing is. I remember when I first noticed that I had difficulty hearing. I work with children, and I realized that I could not hear their soft and higher-pitched voices. Then, slowly, I needed the TV volume to be louder and louder. I remember lying on the pillow next to my wife and not hearing her when she talked to me.

"Are you listening to me?" I heard this question at home and work. I was trying to participate, but I simply could not hear.

Our world is swirling about us. So many sounds. So much noise. So much vitriol and anger. Division and brokenness. Voices are shouting, vying for our attention. Turn on any screen, and the visual and aural information overwhelms you.

Have you ever been having a conversation and you mention something—it could be anything—and later, when you are scrolling on your phone, that thing you were talking about pops up in the form of an ad or a story? Our phones listen better than we do! Scary.

With all the noise swirling around, how do we choose what to hear or who to listen to? What filters do we put in place? So often, we hear the loudest voices, the shouting, and the cacophony of chaos in which we live. And we miss the still, small voice that gives us life.

I hear differently when I am on the trail early in the morning. Or maybe I'm just listening differently. I listen to the song of a warbler on migration. I'll listen and recognize the sound of a mockingbird protecting her nest. I listen to the wind and leaves dancing in the wind. I hear my feet moving in rhythm against the dirt as I go on the trail. Sometimes it is so quiet in the woods, I can hear my own heart beating.

Listening is not something that we do only with our ears. I've written before about how we listen with our hearts. As we establish a sense of calm, we must learn to listen with our ears and hearts. And we must learn to listen with our souls. We must listen to the silence. How often do you hear your heart beating—not in a moment of anxiety, but in silence and peace? You hear the beat of life in your chest.

Sometimes I become so overwhelmed by the silence that I find myself weeping. Have you ever been moved to tears by an unexpected moment of holy silence? I believe that holy silence is there for us to experience, but we simply do not listen.

We also need to listen to each other. Kate Murphy, in her book *You're Not Listening* (2020), frames modern life as particularly antagonistic to good listening: "We are encouraged to listen to our hearts, listen to our inner voices, and listen to our guts, but rarely are we encouraged to listen carefully and with intent to other people."

———

When we purchased our home, one of the things we knew we would have to do would be to replace the windows. Over thirty-year-old single-pane aluminum windows don't keep out the noise—or anything else. We could hear neighbors talking in their backyard or the other neighbor playing her piano. Our home was never silent.

In 2021, we took the big step of replacing the windows. The big, expensive step. We now have beautiful new windows and a silent home. Our home is a place of silence and refuge. Making it that way took intention. It took listening, not just with our ears but with our entire beings. It took turning off whatever was making the noise. The TV, computer, or phone.

Sometimes it also means separating yourself from the toxic voices in your life. If I had done this when I was younger, I could have heard the birds singing earlier in my life. We fail to hear the wind when bombarded by the voices shouting at us. Often, the voice shouting the loudest—the voice I so often ignore—comes from within my soul.

I'm learning to listen to that voice. I'm learning to listen and recognize different bird calls. I'm listening to the wind. I'm learning to listen for that still, small voice that speaks in a whisper.

It's never too late to begin.

INVITATION

This might be the most challenging exercise in my book.

You are invited to sit in silence for two minutes. Then ten minutes. Then an hour. It might take you a day to do this. It might take you a week. Maybe you can't do it at all.

I believe in you, though.

When I say sit in silence, I want you to do your best to find a place without sound—or minimal sound. Maybe you will find a room in the center of your home. Perhaps it's a basement, the bathroom, or in your car. I find solace within the cathedral of the forest. I sit under a tree away from others and listen. I hear the beating of my heart and the rhythm of my breath. I also enjoy the silence of the early morning before the sun makes her bright-eyed appearance.

I see this as a form of meditation—a simple practice accessible to all. Meditation reduces stress, increases calmness and clarity, and promotes positivity. Meditation involves paying close attention to the present moment—especially our own thoughts, emotions, and sensations—whatever it is that's happening. You can practice meditation on your own anytime and anywhere. But listening to basic guided meditations can also be helpful, especially when getting started. There are countless apps that provide this type of guided meditation.

For this exercise, I invite you to simply BE in silence.

> Be STILL and KNOW that I am God.
> Be STILL and KNOW that I am.
> Be STILL and KNOW.
> Be STILL
> BE.
> —Richard Rohr[1]

REFLECTION

- How did this exercise go for you? Was it helpful, or did it increase your frustration?
- Describe this quiet place. (Maybe you can rent it out?)
- How can you build moments of silence into your life?

SUPPLICATION

Christ, be with me—help me to hear. Christ, be with me.
You are.
The still small voice.
The whisper of a loved one.

Snow falling.
A summer breeze.
Bare feet in beach sand.
A goodnight kiss.
A gentle hug.
A wink.
An autumn leaf descending.
A sigh.
A longing.
A memory I cherish.
Christ, be with me—help me to hear. Christ, be with me.
Amen.

15. Grow

Christ be with me—help me to grow. Christ, be with me.

"'Where I am going, you cannot come.' I give you a new commandment, that you love one another. Just as I have loved you, you also should love one another. By this, everyone will know that you are my disciples, if you have love for one another" (John 13:33–35).

"On the one hand, loving one another as Jesus has loved encompasses the mundane; it means serving one another, even in the most menial tasks. This love also encompasses heroic acts of significant risk; it extends even to giving one's life to another."[1]

These words and Jesus's charge offer us what we have seen as a binary way of seeing the world around us. I am going—you cannot come. As I loved you—love one another. Serving others—or giving your life.

I love Easter Day and the fifty days of Easter, of course, and at the same time, I am particularly fond of "Holy Saturday." Holy Saturday—the in-between, the waiting, the fear, the worry, the not knowing what is next, the exhaustion, the grief, the hard work, the silence.

Why is it my favorite? Because the fertile soil of the waiting is rich with change and growth. It takes hard work—blood, sweat, and tears . . . literally. I will do just about anything to get the money shot . . . you know . . . the photo of *that* bird. I remember trying to photograph a painted bunting when I slipped and fell down an embankment. I bruised my ego, scraped my arm . . . but I saved my camera!

Our world is in the midst of a long Holy Saturday. This season not only taught me how to look at the world around me, but also how to see—not just with my eyes, but with my heart.

This season has helped me weather the storms that rage.

In these storms, we fear that the boat might sink. Political storms. Abuse of power. Addiction of all kinds. Covid. Cancer. Economic worries. Injustice. Violence against anyone who thinks or loves differently than we do. Gun violence. Racism. War in Ukraine. A grocery store in Buffalo. A classroom in Uvalde. We pray for those who grieve this day.

Holy Saturday offers the church language for our lived experience here and now during these difficult days. On Holy Saturday, the tomb is sealed tight, the stench of death lingers, and the world waits for a miracle.

The Collect for Holy Saturday reads, "O God, Creator of heaven and earth: Grant that, as the crucified body of your dear Son was laid in the tomb and rested on this holy Sabbath, so we may await with him the coming of the third day, and rise with him to newness of life; who now lives and reigns with you and the Holy Spirit, one God, forever and ever. Amen."[2]

I created a painting for my book *Under the Fig Tree: Visual Prayers and Poems for Lent*. It is a painting of a bare tree. At the base, a rose blooms. Next to the rose is a woman. Maybe Mary. Maybe you. The stars twinkle and shine in the ink-stained night sky. She stands at the base of the winter tree—branches bare and outstretched. She grieves for what has been lost. She longs for what is to be. She remembers his words. At the base of the tree, a flower appears. New life is coming.

One of the ways we mark Holy Saturday at Palmer Memorial Episcopal Church, where I serve in Houston, Texas, is by gathering in the community and planting what we call Easter Grace Gardens. Each participant takes a container, fills it with dark soil, and creates their own garden. Sometimes we plant succulents; other times, we plant marigolds. We designed paths out of gravel, and this past year, we used aquarium fish caves as tombs. The goal is to imagine and create your own version of the garden where Jesus was placed in the tomb and where new life breaks forth on Easter morning. Holy Saturday. Jesus in the tomb. Big and little hands dig in the dirt.

Life comes from darkness.

I still have my garden from last year. The succulents are a bit leggy, and the soil probably needs a bit of fertilizer, but it's still here.

I'm still here. You're still here. And together, we grow.

In my book *My Favorite Color Is Blue. Sometimes.,* I write about growth and the color green.

Green is a promise.
Green is new life.
Green is planting seeds and watching them grow.
Green are the stems of the flowers that make me think of you.
Green are the fields where we played together.
Green are the leaves of our favorite tree dancing in the breeze.
Green is tilling the soil.
Green is the changing of seasons.
Green is learning to trust.
Green is filled with hope.
Green is a new beginning.[3]

INVITATION

You are invited to create your own Easter Grace Garden.

The options, of course, are endless.

Fill a planter with potting soil and set a small, overturned pea pot, or other small container in the dirt to represent Jesus's tomb.

Add a stone to cover the pot's opening like the stone that was rolled in front of the tomb. From there, get creative!

You can fill a small lid with water to create a pond, complete with a floating lily pad. You can add a path with gravel or glass stones or mosaic pieces. Add moss, succulents, and more.

We do this activity with children on Holy Saturday. It can be done any time of the year—and doesn't have to be a faith-based activity.

REFLECTION

- How does working with the earth, hands in the soil, impact your awareness of humanity?
- What did you plant in your garden? Why?
- What things in your life would you consider good fertilizer for the garden of your soul?

SUPPLICATION

Christ, be with me—help me to grow.
Christ, be with me.
I am waiting.
I am always waiting.
Waiting for what?
I don't know.
In my waiting, I miss what happens in the moment.
The seeds that are planted.
The quiet moments of life unfurling.
I miss things because I am waiting.
Help me to be present.
Now.
Help me to celebrate today.
Not tomorrow.

Not next week.
And help me to see that you are the one.
Waiting for me.
Christ, be with me—help me to grow. Christ, be with me.
Amen.

16. TRUTH

Christ, be with me in my truth-telling. Christ, be with me.

It's a great game to play with people you want to get to know better. Hilarity almost always ensues. The game is also as simple as the name suggests. You tell three things about yourself. Two of them are true. One of them is not. The other people must guess which answer is the lie.

Lots of laughter, and you learn how well people lie. What is truth? Truth with a capital "T" or a lowercase "t." In my work as a Christian educator, the children I serve often ask whether the stories we read are true or false.

Actually, I take that back. Young children don't ask that question. The older a child gets, the more they ask that question. The shift is fascinating, and it's hard to put your finger on when this change happens. When do we lose that spirit of wonder? We take stories like Noah's ark and make them into a "cute" anecdote filled with precious pairs of animals, paint them on our nursery walls, and fail to include the fullness of the story.

Have you ever read the full story? Alongside the familiar images of two giraffes, there are the images we don't see. This story is filled with destruction, fear, sadness, and so much loss. I might be a party pooper, but I don't think this is appropriate for nursery walls.

What is the truth in the story of Noah's ark? The answer is especially important when it comes to how we tell all the stories of our faith. There have been countless times when children begin to

understand the fullness of a story like Noah's ark. I see deep con-
fusion and a sudden awareness in their eyes. There is truth in the
story of cute pairs of animals. And there is truth in the story filled
with death and destruction.

As I began to navigate life with the awareness of knowing that
I had anxiety, the truth took on a new meaning. A deeper meaning. Most of the time, I carry myself in a way that people see lots of
joy, confidence, and happiness. I smile a lot. I am very cheerful and
a cup-half-full kind of person. But the way I feel is not always the
way I act. I struggle with a lack of confidence. I'm often unhappy
or sad. And I worry much of the time.

With significant work and evolving self-awareness, I came to
a place where I needed to be honest with myself and those around
me. I'm not always optimistic or happy, and that is OK. Surely, no
one else is either. I create an external persona that hides an internal
reality. A mask that hides my real emotions.

I experienced healing when I removed the mask. I found true
joy, not pretend joy. I found a connection with others who also
struggle with anxiety and depression. And I learned the importance
of forgiveness and grace.

We live in a world where the truth is hard to recognize. Videos
are edited to look natural—a deep-web truth. We edit and change
our faces across our social media platforms so that we—and our
lives—look perfect. We glance in the mirror and don't like what
we see, so we edit, erase, reduce, smooth out, whiten, and change
the way we appear. It's easy to feel overwhelmed when seeking the
truth, especially when it comes to our own body, feelings, and
emotions.

Something else I have come to realize is how often we believe
the lies we tell ourselves.

I'm sure we can all share that experience. Anxiety is the biggest
liar of all. Anxiety does not tell the truth. Anxiety, at the most basic

level, is a sensation that is essential to our existence. It keeps us safe and helps us make thoughtful decisions. But when we give the feeling too much power, we risk telling ourselves lies to make the uncomfortable sentiment go away.

I am particularly taken by the work and writing on the subject of anxiety by Soren Kierkegaard, a nineteenth-century Danish philosopher and theologian, generally recognized as the first existentialist philosopher.

"At times, there is such a noise in my head that it is as though my cranium were being lifted up, it is exactly like when the hobgoblins lift a mountain up a little and then hold a ball and make merry inside," he wrote in his journal in February 1838. He was twenty-four years old.

Kierkegaard saw extreme emotion as a sign of intelligence. "Real depression, like the 'vapors,' is found only in the highest circles, in the former case understood in a spiritual sense," he wrote.

The notion of anxiety/dread/angst for Kierkegaard is "freedom's actuality as the possibility of possibility." Kierkegaard's story of a man standing on the edge of a tall building or cliff expresses this idea beautifully. He feels an aversion to the possibility of falling, but at the same time he has a terrifying impulse to intentionally fling himself over the edge. Having the freedom to choose either causes anxiety or dread. Kierkegaard called this our "dizziness of freedom."[1]

Anxiety tells you to worry. It keeps you up at night. It impacts the love you have for yourself and for others. It tells you that you can't when you can. It makes you feel crazy when you are not. It makes you feel hopeless when there is hope. This will forever be a struggle, but I know I am stronger than my anxiety.

And you are stronger than yours. That is the truth.

INVITATION

You are invited to participate in an exercise where we explore what we share with the world around us and what we hold inside.

You will need a large paper grocery bag, a stack of magazines, scissors, and some glue. Then use the magazines to find words and images that describe what you think people see when they look at you—especially with how you present on a daily basis. When you have a satisfactory list of words, glue them onto the outside of the bag. Finally, do the same for the inside of the bag—however, this time, attach words and images of what people *do not* see. The things about yourself you do not freely share with others.

This is a deeply personal exercise, so *if you need to take a break or put it away until you are in a better place, please do so.*

REFLECTION

- How did this exercise challenge you?
- Which side of the bag was easier to label and why?
- What did you learn about yourself through this activity?

SUPPLICATION

Christ, be with me in my truth-telling. Christ, be with me.
I wear a mask.
I wear many masks.
My happy mask is wearing out.
How familiar it is.
It fits so well.
The mask tells a story.
Of fiction.
Sometimes truth.
Behind the mask is a different story.

I wear so many masks to hide what is real.
To hide what is true.
Why am I afraid to show a sad face when sad?
A tired face when soul-weary?
Crow's feet and brown spots?
I am created in your image.
Unmask me.
Help me to shine.
Christ, be with me in my truth-telling. Christ, be with me.
Amen.

17. Holy

Christ is with me. You said, "It is good." Christ, be with me.

ONE OF MY MOST TREASURED POSSESSIONS IS MY GRANDMOTHER'S
sewing box. It is covered in cheap vinyl or plastic. The colors are
electric orange, yellow, and pea green. A product of the late sixties.
The box opens when you unhook a little brass (faux) latch.

This box is filled with holy treasures. There are medicine
bottles filled with buttons. Zippers of all colors. Thread. Sewing
needles—machine and regular. There are snaps. Elastic that is dry
and brittle. There's a pattern from 1960-something. Safety pins,
scissors, a seam ripper. And most incredible is the smell—the smell
of my childhood. The smell of the little house on the side of a
country road in central Louisiana. The smell of turkey and dress-
ing. The smell of my grandmother.

I try not to open it very often, for I don't want these fragrant
memories to disappear. I have carried this box with me from chapter to chapter, house to house. It is a treasure box worth more than
gold to me.

The simplified definition of holy is "dedicated to God." At the
risk of being called a heathen, I consider my grandmother's sewing
box sacred and holy. And then there are the quilts that my grandmother made.

I am not joking when I say that we have some fifty quilts hand-
stitched by my grandmother. Not one of them would win an award
in a quilting competition, which is perfectly fine with me. That's
not why she made them. Each stitch, each square, and each quilt
was made with love.

Maybe this sounds a bit *precious*—which is not my favorite word. But it's also not a word I take lightly, as there are very few things I would consider precious. But these quilts? Absolutely. Precious. Sacred. Holy.

I am nearing the fifty-year mark, and many of these quilts are older than I am. Some are worn and torn, and for the quilt collectors, this might make you shudder. But for my grandmother, it would make her smile. I fall asleep each night under a weighted blanket. If you haven't tried a weighted blanket, you should. But not very far from me is also one of my grandmother's quilts.

As an artist, I often define the way I paint, or the process of my painting, as *painting as prayer*. My grandmother stitched every stitch with love—she was quilting as prayer. There is no lack of written words about the power and meaning of a quilt. It speaks to being stitched together, different patterns, stories, community, safety, and so much more. Maybe I'm a bit dramatic, but I use words like "holy" to describe many things. I might describe a book as being holy.

I describe the stuffed animal I fell asleep with every night as a child as holy. My friendships are holy. I've seen works of art that take my breath away. These works of art are holy. When I walk the trails at our local park and see a deer looking back at me, I consider this holy. We tend to keep *holy* in the church—in a church building. We reserve it for Sundays. But it wasn't until I saw the holy in the "everyday" that I truly understood its meaning.

When I experienced my mental health crisis, I never expected to fall in love with myself, my soul, and my body. I never considered that I would come to see my mental health crisis as holy. I would have never imagined that the mental health crisis I experienced would be a gift for which I would forever be grateful.

You are a gift. You are sacred and holy—created by the Creator as beautiful and, in God's word, "good." Be open to the holiness that surrounds you, is within you, and is you.

I live and work in the Houston area, and I often see cars with license plates or bumper stickers that have sayings that include: IBBLESD, BLSDBMW, ASKDGOD, BNBLESD, SOBLEST, LVN4JC, ANSDPRR, GDSPLAN, GDLVME, and GDSGIFT. I struggle not to cast judgment, even if I can't help but cringe a little bit. Often, these vehicles are flashy, expensive, and communicate success.

I'm on a mission to reclaim the words "blessed" and "holy." Having financial success, driving a fancy car, and labeling it blessed for all to see is a strange and complicated message. If you don't have those things, if you struggle with financial instability, food instability, housing instability, or if you live a simpler life, work hard, but struggle, is your life not blessed? Is your life not holy?

Of course, not only is your life holy. Your life is blessed in the truest sense of the word.

———————

I often find myself turning to the creation story in the book of Genesis. I am particularly taken with the phrase "And God saw that it was good."

[1]In the beginning when God created the heavens and the earth, [2]the earth was a formless void and darkness covered the face of the deep, while a wind from God swept over the face of the waters. [3]Then God said, "Let there be light"; and there was light. [4]And God saw that the light was good; and God separated the light from the darkness. [5]God called the light Day, and the darkness he called Night. And there was evening and there was morning, the first day.

[6]And God said, "Let there be a dome in the midst of the waters, and let it separate the waters from the waters." [7]So God made the dome and separated the waters that were under the dome from the waters that were above the dome. And it was so. [8]God called the dome Sky. And there was evening and there was morning, the second day.

[9]And God said, "Let the waters under the sky be gathered together into one place, and let the dry land appear." And it was so. [10]God called the dry land Earth, and the waters that were gathered together he called Seas. And God saw that it was good. [11]Then God said, "Let the earth put forth vegetation: plants yielding seed, and fruit trees of every kind on earth that bear fruit with the seed in it." And it was so. [12]The earth brought forth vegetation: plants yielding seed of every kind, and trees of every kind bearing fruit with the seed in it. And God saw that it was good. [13]And there was evening and there was morning, the third day.

[14]And God said, "Let there be lights in the dome of the sky to separate the day from the night; and let them be for signs and for seasons and for days and years, [15]and let them be lights in the dome of the sky to give light upon the earth." And it was so. [16]God made the two great lights—the greater light to rule the day and the lesser light to rule the night—and the stars. [17]God set them in the dome of the sky to give light upon the earth, [18]to rule over the day and over the night, and to separate the light from the darkness. And God saw that it was good. [19]And there was evening and there was morning, the fourth day.

[20]And God said, "Let the waters bring forth swarms of living creatures, and let birds fly above the earth across the dome of the sky." [21]So God created the great sea monsters

and every living creature that moves, of every kind, with which the waters swarm, and every winged bird of every kind. And God saw that it was good. ²²God blessed them, saying, "Be fruitful and multiply and fill the waters in the seas, and let birds multiply on the earth." ²³And there was evening and there was morning, the fifth day.

²⁴And God said, "Let the earth bring forth living creatures of every kind: cattle and creeping things and wild animals of the earth of every kind." And it was so. ²⁵God made the wild animals of the earth of every kind, and the cattle of every kind, and everything that creeps upon the ground of every kind. And God saw that it was good.

²⁶Then God said, "Let us make humankind in our image, according to our likeness; and let them have dominion over the fish of the sea, and over the birds of the air, and over the cattle, and over all the wild animals of the earth, and over every creeping thing that creeps upon the earth."

²⁷So God created humankind in his image,
in the image of God he created them;
male and female he created them.

²⁸God blessed them, and God said to them, "Be fruitful and multiply, and fill the earth and subdue it; and have dominion over the fish of the sea and over the birds of the air and over every living thing that moves upon the earth." ²⁹God said, "See, I have given you every plant yielding seed that is upon the face of all the earth, and every tree with seed in its fruit; you shall have them for food. ³⁰And to every beast of the earth, and to every bird of the air, and to everything that creeps on the earth, everything that has the breath of life, I have given every green plant for food." And it was so. ³¹God saw everything that he had made, and

indeed, it was very good. And there was evening and there was morning, the sixth day.

God created you, and you are holy and good!

INVITATION

Houston has one of the most fantastic museum districts in the country. Not a mile down the street is one of the world's most impressive art collections. Houston might get a bad rap, but it's a truly amazing city—especially when it comes to art.

You are invited to go to your local art museum, gallery, etc., and set aside some time to observe the artwork through the lens of looking for the holy. Is there a painting, sculpture, or photograph that touches you in such a way that you catch your breath—that you experience a reaction like awe and wonder? Maybe it takes you to a place of deep grief or anger. In my experience, I would call any of these sentiments the experience of recognizing something holy—whatever that looks like for you.

I remember the moment I came face-to-face with *Fiat Lux* (1963) by Hans Hoffman. Hans Hofmann, born on March 21, 1880, is best known for his energetic and intensely colored art-work. According to his Foundation: "From his early landscapes of the 1930s, to his 'slab' paintings of the late 1950s, and his abstract works at the end of his career upon his death in 1966, Hofmann continued to create boldly experimental color combinations and formal contrasts that transcended genre and style."[1]

Fiat Lux means "Let there be light"—and it most certainly lives up to its name. It takes my breath away.

I experience God as Creator. I experience God as the artist that had to create. Not some Picasso in the sky, but a God of deep longing and creative love.

REFLECTION

- Describe the work of art that most impacted you as part of this exercise.
- What about this exchange between the art and the observer applies to your experience with the holy?

SUPPLICATION

Christ is with me. You said, "It is good."
Christ, be with me.
All of creation is good.
This is what you said.
And then you rested.
I do not feel good today.
I am anxious and afraid.
I long for rest.
I long for peace.
I long for you.
And you are here.
Now.
I'm ready to feel good.
But the world tells me I am no good.
The world tells me I am not worthy.
Help me to listen to you.
And not the world.
You said creation is good.
I am good.
Christ is with me. You said, "It is good."
Christ, be with me.
Amen.

18. STRONG

Christ, be with me. I'm not feeling brave. Christ, be with me.

HOW DO YOU DEFINE BRAVERY? SOME MIGHT SAY IT MEANS NOT BEING afraid of anything. Personally, I think that's the wrong answer.

There is a difference between bravery and fearlessness. We can also be scared and brave at the same time. Feeling or experiencing fear is part of becoming brave. Becoming brave is learning to tolerate that fear we are feeling.

Some people are brave from the earliest age. Not me! In fact, I'm a scaredy-cat, but I have come a long way in finding my brave. "According to research by Jerome Kagan at Harvard University, nearly one out of five babies is born with an inhibited temperament. Fortunately, temperament can be modified by experience. Kagan found that two-thirds of inhibited babies didn't become shy toddlers. These kids become less fearful as they learn to cope."[1]

Middle school field day. The Louisiana heat moved and danced across the pavement—an apparition from hell. Running. Sweating. Competition. Awards. Or not. Teams. Ugh.

My turn came to run the fifty-yard dash. I didn't have the words for it then like I do now, but I was most likely in an anxiety-induced panic attack. I started running. So far, so good. I could see the finish line. Sweat poured into my eyes. And then, my body failed me. I was running full speed toward the finish line when I shit my pants in front of the entire middle school.

Yes, you read that correctly. At that moment, I decided to keep running. Across the finish line, through the playground, and into the school. I had no idea where I was going or what to do, but I knew I had to get away. My eyes burned with tears and shame. Thinking everyone was outside, I ran into my classroom to hide.

Ms. Bailey was there.

Most of what happened next was a blur, but I remember this. Ms. Bailey caught me as I tried to run out of the room, wrapped her arms around me, and pulled me into her lap. Dirty pants and all.

"What's wrong, baby?" she asked, hugging me close.

Through snotty and shame-filled tears, I told her. I thought she would express disgust and throw me off her lap. But, instead, she didn't even flinch. She hugged me tightly and told me she loved me and that everything would be OK. Then, she helped me clean up, found some clean underwear and shorts to put on, and made me go back outside. She even told me I was brave and strong.

I was amazed. A woman I had little in common with became my protector. A doting mother hen, she pulled me to her bosom and held me there until I could breathe again. I remember how safe I felt in her softness—not only softness of body, but of heart. I hope I told her, "Thank you."

Now, when I feel unsafe or afraid, I think of my mom, Mammaw, Ms. Bailey, and Kristin, my beloved partner and wife. Each of these women has held me, loved me, protected me, nourished me, and cared for me.

Feeling safe and protected is imperative in this world we live in. And yet, so many of us do not feel safe and protected. Far too many are not safe and protected. As we seek a calm spirit for our lives, I encourage you to reflect on what it means to be protected and the protector.

After middle school, I lost track of Ms. Bailey. But that doesn't mean I don't feel her presence. That doesn't mean when weary or afraid and falling into God's open arms, I don't see the face or feel the softness of Ms. Bailey enveloping me.

––––––––––

I love a good hero story.

In sagging blue tights and wrinkled red cape, I, along with many of you (Don't be shy!), would leap over tall buildings, save the pretty woman from the evil villain, and come crashing down onto our collective childhood bedroom floors with a loud thud. I would then climb back up on the bed, hold my cape out, stare straight ahead, and take flight . . . if only for an instant. Superman was my hero. He had superpowers and he was a ladies man . . . *and* he could still be cool even when wearing tights!

And then, Superman broke his neck.

How could this be? Superman was able to fly over mountains, zoom through the ocean, and soar through space. Superman even stopped a meteorite from destroying the earth. He did this with his own bare hands. While riding a horse, Superman broke his neck. His body came crashing down. Only this time, he could not get back up.

It seemed as if the evil villain might win.

I fear that we have turned God into Superman. We are so quick to call on God to rescue us, to save us from the evil villain, to appear, cape and all, only when we need God . . . and then, when something goes wrong, or when we feel that God has failed us, we take God and angrily throw God back into the toy box and pull God out again when we are ready to play.

I thought that evil was going to win. Superman was never going to fly again.

What will we ever do? . . . *and* then he was there . . . in a wheelchair, body broken, red cape put away. Superman was back and he was ready to fight. He was not going to let evil win. He was not going to let the world forget about people who, like himself, may never walk (or fly) again. He became the voice—*their* voice—and it was hope that took flight. That is when he became *real*.

Not until body broken, spirit exhausted did God become *real* and walk among us. Superman was put back on the shelf for another day, and Jesus came and dwelt among us. There was no special lighting, make-up, or body doubles.

Let's be real. Let's not look only to the sky for rescue. Let's look into the faces of our brothers and sisters, and there we will see the true definition of courage.[2]

INVITATION

Courage doesn't always look like it might in the movies or in a fairy tale. Courage doesn't always have big muscles and a chiseled jaw. Courage is often quiet and tender. There are countless examples of this type of courage. These are folks who do what's right, and they keep doing it, regardless of the risk to themselves or their personal self-interest. There are some we might recognize by name—Mary Oliver, poet, and Georgia O'Keeffe, painter. But, of course, they don't have to be famous.

You are invited to approach this day with a simple mantra— "Today, I choose to live with courage." You are also invited to come up with a mantra or affirmation of your own choosing.

REFLECTION

- Think back to when you were a child. Who was your role model for bravery or courage?
- How does courage—or lack thereof—impact your mental health?
- What is one thing you can do today that takes courage?

SUPPLICATION

Christ, be with me. I'm not feeling brave.
Christ, be with me.
Help me to be Ms. Bailey in the world.
Open arms.
Comforting words.
Understanding.
Soft place to land.
But how do I do this when I do not feel brave?
How do I do this when I do not feel like I am enough?
You are brave.
You carried the weight of the world to your death.
Help me remember that you were also afraid.
You wept.
You cried out in agony.
"Take this cup from me!"
And you were brave.
Thank you, Jesus, for carrying my fear.
Help me understand yours.
I am working each day to be braver.
I am working each day to be like you.
Christ, be with me. I'm not feeling brave.
Christ, be with me.
Amen.

19. Home

Christ, be with me. I'm on my way home. Christ, be with me.

Between birth and age seventeen, I lived in eleven different trailers/apartments/houses in six cities and three states. That is an average of six and a half months in each house. Less than three years in each city. And less than six years in each state.

Until I started writing this book, I had never actually written any of this down—but how freeing it is to finally put everything on paper. Beyond the moves, we also experienced just about every other hardship a family can encounter. Financial instability. Food insecurity. Divorce. Illness. Job insecurity. Remarriage. Adoption. Addiction. Clergy family. Clergy moves.

All the things.

I have not had the easiest life. And I've had a beautiful life.

I love my mom and papa. They did everything they could to provide us stability in the good and hard times. I love my wife. She carries me. Loves me. Protects me.

I realize I'm not the only person struggling with the definition of home. Home might be where you eat most of your meals or fall asleep at night. Home can be family. Yet, family is not where you find home for many of you. Maybe this is an oversimplification or a stretch, but let's take an expansive view of what home might mean.

Open house. Broken home. *Home is where the heart is.* That last one makes me gag a little.

Home sweet home.

Home is where you gather. And again, for many, home is not where you gather or want to gather. For those trying to find their way home, there's an equal number of people running away from home. For me, home has been an apartment, a mobile home, a rental home, a rectory, a dorm room, our first home that took forever to sell, and a home whose foundation failed.

Home is in the arms of my beloved. Home is in the woods when I'm alone with my thoughts. For far too many, home is the streets. Under a bridge. In a tent. The shelter.

So, trying to define home is nearly impossible. It is all of this and more, and it is none of this.

I am particularly interested in what it means to be at home in our bodies. For our bodies are all we really have, right? Bodies are incredible. The human body is complex, varied, beautiful, wounded, healed, broken, active, anxious, sick, calm, tired, sad, joyful, and so much more.

I believe you are taking a positive step in becoming more at home in your body by reading this book. When I made my body a priority, I experienced a spirit of calm and hopefulness where for so long there was little.

The world does not offer the best advice for being at home in our own skin.

We are too fat, too skinny, too tall, too short, too black, too white, too different, too feminine, too masculine, too gay, too religious, too wild, too dull, too conservative, too liberal, too little, too much, too late. On my good days, I can shut out these messages. And I have lots of good days. I also have days when those messages create anxiety, fear, hurt, and brokenness.

Let's look with fresh eyes at the saying, "Home is where the heart is." Your heart is beating in your chest and in your body. Home is where the heart is.

My prayer for you and me is one in which we can look at our reflection in the mirror, see ourselves and all our perfect imperfections, and be able to say welcome home—and mean it.

INVITATION

You are invited to explore the "floorplan" of your heart.

I want you to push the bounds of your creativity just a bit with this one. Imagine that your heart has a floor plan—an entrance, different rooms, closets, hidden rooms, a basement, hallways, etc. Draw the floor plan and label each room/space.

Maybe your heart has lots of windows that open to the world. Maybe your heart has no windows and is closed off. Perhaps the kitchen is enormous—a central space where hospitality is a priority. Maybe the tiny hall closet is filled with grief.

Where is faith found on this floor plan? Is it the foundation? The framework? Or is it nowhere to be found?

REFLECTION

- How did this exercise challenge your view of how you imagined your interior life?
- What surprised you?
- What needs renovating or shoring up?

SUPPLICATION

Christ, be with me. I'm on my way home.
Christ, be with me.
No GPS or AAA TripTik will lead me home.
Not to the home I am searching for.
I have a house.
It has rooms, and windows, and love.
And still, I search for home.
What am I searching for?
I watch the mother bird feed her young.
Preparing them to leave home.

To leave the nest.
What if I don't want to leave the nest?
What if I am afraid to fly?
Maybe leaving home means coming home.
Maybe coming home means trusting in you.
Maybe home is now.
Christ, be with me. I'm on my way home.
Christ, be with me.
Amen.

20. FORGIVE

Christ, be with me. I'm learning to forgive. Christ, be with me.

IT'S NOT IMPOSSIBLE, BUT ONE OF THE HARDEST THINGS FOR ME TO DO is not only forgive others but also forgive myself. It is as if a jury lives inside my mind and chooses a guilty verdict each time.

I guess I can say that I am working on it.

When you've been hurt, particularly by a friend, a colleague, or a family member, the tendency is to hold on to the hurt and let it flavor all future interactions. Another thing that happens is that the hurt inflicted also changes your perception of the past. So, at least, I will look back over the relationship and start picking it apart—finding divisions or slights that weren't there—especially if it is someone you love and care for deeply.

The spiral can make you feel like you are drowning.

There are people in my life that I need to forgive. There are people in my life that need to forgive me. Why is this such difficult work?

When the recipe for the pain includes many different ingredients, forgiveness gets especially complicated. My recipe includes ego, broken trust, extreme sensitivity, and more. And it certainly isn't as tasty as homemade bread or chocolate chip cookies. This recipe creates something dense and heavy. It weighs down my heart and my soul.

This pain creates heartbreak.

So, where do we begin to find relief? Right where it hurts the most: within our hearts and souls. We must do the work to forgive ourselves. This work is not for the faint of heart. Brave work requires you to have the right tools in your tool bag.

Let's take a deep dive into something that has become a daily occurrence in the mind of Roger. It all starts with a tool bag—one with a hammer, screwdriver, and all the other tools you need in one place.

One morning, I needed a hammer. So, I went to the garage where my tool bag was kept. Funny enough, it wasn't there. After a bit of head scratching and looking around, I found it. I opened the bag, but the hammer wasn't there. Neither was the screwdriver.

I started digging around the garage and couldn't find any of my tools. I wished I could have blamed the situation on others. But I couldn't. It's all me. It is the way Roger moves through life. Now I'm forced to go from room to room, opening junk drawers, and looking high and low, but nothing turns up. I give up, go outside to watch the birds in the backyard, and reflect on how I spend more time looking for things than getting actual work done. The bird feeders are empty, so I take them down to fill them and discover a hammer, *the* hammer, on the ground in the backyard, where I last used it.

Why didn't I put that hammer back where I found it? And what does this have to do with forgiveness? Well, after forgiving myself for the mishap, I realize that, when it comes to forgiveness, a variety of emotion and spiritual tools are necessary. Our toolbox needs to be filled with time, patience, rest, nourishment, therapy, grace, and humor, to name just a few.

There are people in my life that I am unable to forgive. The hurt they inflicted on both me and those I love remains so painful the wounds might never heal. But I've often wondered what happens if the wounds do in fact remain forever? Because we can go to our graves with these wounds still wide open, we must practice forgiveness as an act of emotional triage to have any hope of transcending the pain we still carry.

And this begins with naming what those wounds are. Of course, I can't tell you to forgive everyone who has hurt you. I simply do not believe such a thing is realistic, possible, or even recommended. That doesn't mean, however, we can't tend to our wounds and to the wounds of others. For, when we do this, healing occurs.

I remember a time when I learned I had hurt someone deeply. It was a shock because I did not realize I had hurt them. I had wondered why our relationship had changed but couldn't come up with a reason. So finally, I decided to ask, and this friend was brave enough to tell me.

I'd like to say that I'm a good listener. And I am sometimes, but not all the time. This person shared something with me in the past that I ignored or discounted. When I realized I had done this, I asked for forgiveness, and they obliged. I felt so much lighter, and our friendship continues to this day.

Let's look back at my toolbox.

Kind of like the hammer, the thing I have the most difficulty finding when searching for forgiveness is patience. I have never been a patient person, and it's been problematic for me in more ways than one.

For those familiar with an author's life in the trenches of the publishing world, you know that patience is imperative, or you will have the most difficult of times. Writing and publishing a book is a lot like raising a child. In the early stages, it's exhilarating and frequently a little smelly. There are tears and tantrums, celebrations, and rituals. And there are disappointments and mistakes, as well as growth and change. There are arguments and discussions within yourself and with the child.

One moment you stand in awe of this child, and then there are those dark nights of the soul when you wonder if you are cut out for this parenting thing. There are parts you want to erase and moments so riveting that you lose yourself.

Writing a book takes significant commitment and loads of patience. A seed is planted. It must be tended, cared for, and loved. Then one day, you are holding the book in your hand and realize that you will never be the same.

In my experience, forgiveness has been quite similar. Sure, I'd like to say that you can look to me as a role model for how to forgive and be forgiven. But I'm a work in progress, and I bet you are too.

It has taken a long time to get here, but I am on the path of forgiving myself. And that path is really a journey, especially when you are working on yourself.

Remember, it's OK if it takes a little time or a lifetime. Just know that it is happening.

Now, where is that damn hammer?

INVITATION

You are invited to list what tools you want in your mental health toolbox—especially the tools needed when working toward forgiveness. Get creative!

My toolbox might include a small notebook, various art supplies, writing utensils, a healthy snack, a bottle of water, kind and encouraging messages from friends, and photos of those I love.

One idea might be to assign specific tools jobs based on their current purpose—for example, a level to level out your moods, a hammer to hammer an idea in, or a measuring tape that helps to measure your thoughts or reactions.

REFLECTION

- What tools are you missing from your mental health toolbox? What can you do to add them to your collection? Where do you find them?
- What tools do you need when working on forgiveness? Is there a relationship that needs repair? Are there expectations that need adjusting?

SUPPLICATION

Christ, be with me. I'm learning to forgive.
Christ, be with me.
Turn the other cheek.
That's what you said.
Are you kidding me?
I do not want to turn the other cheek.
Sometimes, I want to lash out.
I want to inflict pain.
I am defensive.
I am angry.
I want to hurt the person in front of me.
And I do.
I say things that are mean.
I say things that are not true, but I still say them.
I should forgive them.
They look back at me.
From the mirror.
Longing for forgiveness.
Christ, be with me. I'm learning to forgive.
Christ, be with me.
Amen.

21. FRIEND

Christ, be with me. I need a friend. Christ, be with me.

I WOULD NOT BE HERE TODAY IF IT WEREN'T FOR THE FRIENDS I HAVE made throughout my lifetime, but, when I was teenager, there was only one other person my age I could call a friend. Now, if you think I am being dramatic and underestimating the number of friends I had, you're wrong. I absolutely did not have many friends growing up.

Sure, I had Miss Bailey, Mr. Shelby, Mr. Gingles, and maybe a few other adult friends. But, of course, teachers serve a different purpose than buddies. When we are younger, adults are there to teach, lead, and take responsibility for our safety. Friends our age make us feel less alone, and my one friend was extraordinary at doing that and so much more.

I've written about him before and will continue to tell his story. I promised him I would.

He escaped to the United States with his family because of Cambodia's political unrest and war. My dad was rector of the church extending hospitality and welcome to this family. I remember the first time I saw Suth. Everything about him was so different from me. I remember his coal-black hair and gentle demeanor.

As a teenager, I often felt like an outsider. He was an outsider. And we clicked. We became brothers. We spent so much time together—talking, laughing, and fishing. Our common language was not English. It was fishing.

When I was newly married, living in Myrtle Beach, South Carolina, and he was in school in California, he got sick. Very sick. Diagnosed with brain cancer, he died not long after.

I still feel that loss in my bones. It is an achingly profound loss that will never stop haunting me. My heart was shattered. He was here for such a short time—yet he taught me so much.

I go to the lake to fish, to pray . . . and to be with my friend. I see him in the sparkling water. I sense his presence in the thrill of catching a fish. He is with me. Always. I hear his voice on the wind.

Often, I wonder if our friendship would still be strong today. Would we still go fishing? Would he have a family and children? One thing I know for sure is he would have changed the world. He certainly changed mine. In fact, that's why I'm convinced he's still with and around me.

While writing this book, I have discovered that many of my friendships have something in common—water and the love of nature, beauty, and creation—especially the holiness of creation.

I've mentioned in past chapters that I am a photographer. When Covid hit, and after wearing out the soles of at least three pairs of tennis shoes, I purchased the best camera possible with my little budget. Little did I know how much this purchase would impact my life.

I would often begin my day with an early morning drive. One spring morning, I discovered Cullinan Park Conservancy. Encompassing 750 acres of prairie and woodlands, Cullinan Park is one of the largest nature parks in the Houston area. It contains an observation tower, countless nature trails, a lake, boardwalk, scenic overlook, bird drip (an area set aside for birds that includes water features and native foliage, providing them with fresh water and safe perches), creek, and much more. Cullinan Park became my Eden.

I had my new camera with me and was taking pictures of water birds when I met another photographer. We quickly became friends. Then I met another photographer and another one. Then another. I have made some incredible friendships. Now we bushwhack, fight fire ants together, and eat junk food from Buc-ee's as we drive across the state chasing birds.

One early Monday morning, I showed up to the park where I saw a photographer friend by himself. He usually comes with another buddy of his on a different day. He was alone. I could also tell by his body language that something was going on.

I asked him how he was doing.

His response caught me off guard.

"Not good," he said. "I had to put my dog down last night." He was broken and grieving, having also lost his wife in recent years.

I put my hand on his shoulder, hoping I had said what he needed to hear.

Trevor and I remain friends. We often walk the trail together, comparing photographs and sharing stories. Same goes for Allen, Chris, Cin-Ty, Clarence, Gary, Henry, Jerzey, Karla, Keith, Robbin, Sandy, Sr. Mary, Susanne, Tena, and so many others.

We all became so close that when I had the flu and didn't show up for a few days, I got wind that there were lots of "Where is Roger?" conversations on the dock. I also received several texts— one asking if I had been eaten by an alligator. I was missed, and being missed felt good. I missed my friends too!

I've also made some long-lasting friendships through my work in the Church—with clergy, staff colleagues, youth ministry members, conference and camp friends. The list goes on.

We are there for each other in difficult times and in times of celebration.

While true friendship is one of life's greatest gifts, ceasing to be friends with a person is one of its most challenging moments. Why do these endings hurt so much?

And then there are friendships that you thought were everlasting. They sometimes end too, and you don't know why.

I have a friend from college with whom I was inseparable. We began our college career together in the same first-year-student seminar. She was an artist. I am an artist. She was like a sister. We laughed together. Made cheesy mixed tapes for each other. We spent Friday nights eating at Woolworths in Asheville, North Carolina. It was never a romantic relationship; we were simply good friends.

For a while after graduation, we stayed in touch. I certainly made the effort. It's been years since we've talked, and I miss her. I send her a message every couple of years just wishing her well. Maybe she will read this book and reach out to me. I'd like that. But, like with anything, friendships change and grow. Friendships end. Friendships have a life of their own.

I decided to write a chapter about friendship because I'm not sure I'd be here without my friends. In my darkest moments, when afraid, hurting, or grieving, my friends hold me up. Even when I am hard to take. Roger is a lot on a good day. But Roger on a lousy day is damn near impossible.

Yet, they stick with me. They hold me accountable. They call me out. I listen to what they have to say. They challenge me. They inspire me. And some of them still laugh until tears roll down their faces when I tell those darn poop stories as if we are twelve years old.

INVITATION

You are invited to reach out to a friend and tell them what they mean to you.

If you love them, let them know. If they have encouraged you without knowing it, let them know. Let them know if they have impacted your life in ways they may not be aware of.

In 2021, I did just this with a number of friends and family members I had lost contact with. We would occasionally "like" each other's posts on Facebook, but it wasn't a deep and emotional reconnection. So I wrote letters—handwritten letters where I poured out my gratitude and love for them. I highlighted special memories I had, and thanked them for loving me. The impact of these letters went deeper than I ever could imagine.

Maybe you are struggling with a friendship. Perhaps that friendship is changing or is damaged. Maybe this friendship has become toxic, and it is time for it to end. Closure isn't necessarily the easiest thing to initiate, but it is often one of the best things for everyone involved.

REFLECTION

- What words best describe your friendships? What images?
- How do your friendships change as you get older?
- Where, on your list of priorities, are your friends? Do they take a lot of work, or are they easy—comfortable?

SUPPLICATION

Christ, be with me. I need a friend. Christ, be with me.
I have many friends.
Why do I feel so alone?
Do you ever feel alone?
Do you ever get tired of us asking things of you?
Do you ever tire of our selfishness and ego?
Do you have any friends?
Or does everyone just want a piece of you?

I want to be your friend.

I know which box you checked.

So long ago on that road to Golgatha.

You checked yes.

You will be my friend.

You need a friend too.

Christ, be with me. I need a friend. Christ, be with me.

Amen.

22. Prayer

Christ, be with me. My life is a prayer. Christ, be with me.

My earliest memories of praying were around the kitchen table at my grandparents' home. It was simply what we did before we ate. Not until I wrote this book, however, did I realize I had never heard my grandmother pray with words at the dinner table. It was always my grandfather or another man.

Using words is just one of many ways we can pray. My grandmother prayed by preparing a colorful and delicious meal for her family. She took the bounty God gave her and prepared it for those she loved the most. Cooking and quilting were central to her life— they were also her ways of praying.

A couple of times, Suth, my friend from Cambodia, came along on a visit to my grandparents' home. During one of those visits, following lunch, we observed him go to the kitchen and come back into the living room with his plate—several times.

My grandparents hand-washed all the dishes, so we told him to put his plate by the sink so they could wash it. He looked at us as if he felt ill and said that every time he went to take his dish and put it by the sink, she would put more food on it, and he did not know how to say no!

We still laugh at that story.

Hospitality through food was another way my grandmother prayed. Actions, not words. Even though I am a writer, I struggle with praying with words. I get distracted, self-edit what I'm saying, or fall asleep. I often feel a disconnect when I come to the one I pray to. But I didn't realize that I had been communicating with God—and God with me—all along. Prayer took the form of creative expression, be it painting, photography, or writing.

It's true.

Late one evening, after working on a painting, I decided I hated it and wanted to throw it away. I threw my brushes into the trash and started to toss the canvas away. But I didn't. I felt drawn to squeeze paint from the tubes directly onto the canvas. And then, I put my fingers into the color and began moving the paint around. At one point, I looked at the clock and realized it was three in the morning, and I had been painting with my fingers for hours.

I will never forget the moment when I realized that I had communicated with the Holy through finger painting.

I was painting as a prayer.

Earlier this year, I released a book titled *Sparrow's Prayer*.

The story is about a little sparrow who wakes up one morning and finds his words tangled in his beak like old yarn and straw. He normally begins his day by thanking God. On this day, he cannot find the words. He seeks help from a few of his friends. Turtle needs help getting blackberries to make a blackberry pie for Fox. Mousy is working on a painting and needs Sparrow's help choosing a color for the sky. And Buck wants to dance with Sparrow, but Sparrow feels like birds can't dance. After three simple encounters, Sparrow realizes he's been living his life all day as a prayer of thanksgiving. It changes how he looks at prayer and how he practices prayer. Prayer becomes embodied within him, bringing him closer to the Creator.

A chapter on embodied prayer may seem a little out of place in a book like this. Yet I believe it fits perfectly. Prayer centers me. Prayer provides space for silence and listening. Prayer is words, and prayer is dancing. Prayer is hands outstretched. Prayer is hands covered in paint. Prayer is song. Prayer is welcoming the stranger. Prayer gives voice to our anxieties and fears. Prayer gives voice to our joy and gratitude.

If you look up the definition of prayer in the dictionary, you might find words like "a solemn request for help or expression of thanks addressed to God."[1] You might also see words like invocation, intercession, and devotion. Prayer doesn't have to be solemn. Prayer can be filled with excitement and joy. It can also be filled with deep pain and grief.

I hope you will take from this chapter the knowledge and self-awareness that you are living your life as a prayer by simply being you. God is listening and wants you to know you are loved. Amen.

INVITATION

I once taught a class with my friend Neil called "Painting the Psalms." The class was one I'll never forget. Neil would pick a psalm from the Bible and offer a reflection on the meaning and structure of the psalm. He is a word guy.

Following the discussion about the psalm, I would invite participants to create a painting based on what they heard in the psalm. Remarkably, everyone's artwork focused on different parts of the psalm. Painting the Psalms enabled the participant to "break open" the psalm in new ways.

You are invited to do the same. Pick a psalm. A good one might be Psalm 139:1–18. Read it. Reread it. Then create a painting based on what you carry after reading it.

O LORD, you have searched me and known me.
You know when I sit down and when I rise up;
you discern my thoughts from far away.
You search out my path and my lying down,
and are acquainted with all my ways.
Even before a word is on my tongue,
O LORD, you know it completely.

You hem me in, behind and before,
and lay your hand upon me.
Such knowledge is too wonderful for me;
it is so high that I cannot attain it.
Where can I go from your spirit?
Or where can I flee from your presence?
If I ascend to heaven, you are there;
if I make my bed in Sheol, you are there.
If I take the wings of the morning
and settle at the farthest limits of the sea,
even there your hand shall lead me,
and your right hand shall hold me fast.
If I say, "Surely the darkness shall cover me,
and the light around me become night,"
even the darkness is not dark to you;
the night is as bright as the day,
for darkness is as light to you.
For it was you who formed my inward parts;
you knit me together in my mother's womb.
I praise you, for I am fearfully and wonderfully made.
Wonderful are your works;
that I know very well.
My frame was not hidden from you,
when I was being made in secret,
intricately woven in the depths of the earth.
Your eyes beheld my unformed substance.
In your book were written
all the days that were formed for me,
when none of them as yet existed.
How weighty to me are your thoughts, O God!
How vast is the sum of them!
I try to count them—they are more than the sand;
I come to the end—I am still with you.

REFLECTION

- What is your main takeaway from the psalm you chose and the painting you created?
- Did engaging with the psalm through art help you to experience it in a new or more profound way?

SUPPLICATION

Christ, be with me. My life is a prayer.
Christ, be with me.
Painters paint.
This is prayer.
Dancers dance.
This is prayer.
Kindness is prayer.
Listening is prayer.
Crying is prayer.
Holding space is prayer.
Righteous anger is prayer.
Silence is prayer.
Kneeling is prayer.
Reaching is prayer.
Serving is prayer.
Hope is prayer.
Rest is prayer.
My life is prayer.
Christ, be with me. My life is a prayer.
Christ, be with me.
Amen.

23. HOPE

Christ, be with me. May I be a hope-bearer. Christ, be with me.

IN THE DEPTHS OF MY MENTAL HEALTH CRISIS IN 2017, I *KNEW* I WAS not OK. I *knew* that my world had fallen apart and could never be put back together. I was sure of it.

Shows you how much I knew.

I would lie in bed and sob at night because I had lost all hope. Let me repeat that. I had lost *all* hope. But where did it go? Where was cheerful Roger? Where was grateful Roger? Where was hopeful Roger?

As human beings moving through this life, we will, without fail, experience the highest of highs and the lowest of lows. There are seasons in our lives when things can be challenging. Somewhere along the way, I had lost myself and, along with it, any sense of optimism for the future.

Why is hope so important? In my experience, because it reduces feelings of helplessness. Hope increases happiness, reduces stress, and improves our quality of life.

When I gave anxiety the power to take charge, I not only lost hope but also sight of important goals I had set for myself. Challenges were piling up in my life as a parent and citizen in a country that I had trouble recognizing. Crushing financial struggles and scary health struggles certainly didn't help either. I failed to set boundaries and live within those boundaries. I didn't see a path through to the other side. I couldn't even imagine or wonder what might be on the other side. I was stuck, afraid, and hopeless.

As I began to intentionally focus on my health and wellness, not only physically but spiritually and mentally, I learned that hope is a muscle we must exercise. It is not something we are necessarily predisposed to, so we must work that muscle for it to gain spiritual strength and traction.

I experienced a return to hope when I returned to the community. I experienced hope when I walked and felt the sun on my skin. I experienced hope when I found myself laughing again. I experienced hope when I returned to painting after stepping away from it for a couple of years.

I don't want this chapter to seem like having hope will end all struggle. That is impossible. There will always be a struggle. Hope is a way of thinking that pushes us into action. Hope is about what is possible. Hope is about envisioning a moment in the future different from the moment at hand. Hope improves our physical health, our mental health, and spiritual health. Hope improves our relationships.

Hope implies that there is the possibility of a better future, according to the famed hope researcher C. R. Snyder. It shows up at the worst possible time when things are dire and difficult, but can keep us going during those hard moments. If during the difficulty, we can see the faint glimmer of something better, then hope "opens us up," says Barbara Fredrickson, a positive psychology researcher.[1]

Having hope helps me to manage my stress and anxiety. Hope helps me set goals, and sometimes I even meet those goals! In 2020, I began taking daily walks. I hoped it would help me navigate quarantine and become healthier. Having hope helped these goals to come true.

Hope helps me feel happier. Hope shows me that I am strong. Hope gives me wings to fly.

Have you ever been around someone who has lost hope? It is heartbreaking. We must not lose hope. Hope is sustaining and transforming.

INVITATION

You are invited to create a different painting representing your life pre-Covid, before your mental health struggles, loss, or other difficult transition.

Let the painting dry, then turn it over.

Now . . . tear it up into little pieces.

This activity may elicit an emotional response—you may feel several different emotions. Be gentle and patient with yourself. Do not push or ridicule yourself. Participate in this activity only if you feel grounded and safe.

Life is filled with brokenness and may not look like what we imagined, especially after a loss or transition.

This exercise helps us to know that it is possible to create something beautiful out of these torn pieces. This new creation may include all the torn pieces. Other times, there is beauty in a singular piece, and we hold on to it like a cherished memory.

We—and our lives—are a new creation.

REFLECTION

- How did you feel when you realized that you would have to tear up your painting?
- Describe how creating a new work out of the torn art pieces can be applied to your life today?

SUPPLICATION

Christ, be with me. May I be a hope-bearer.
Christ, be with me.
I am called to be a hope-bearer.
I carry it on my shoulders and in my heart.
Sometimes I can't find it.
Hope is often lost.
Then, there it is when you least expect it.
It appears when you are ready to give up.
I am a hope-bearer.
You are a hope-bearer.
I reach out my hand and take yours.
You bring me under the shelter of your wings.
You help me to feel brave.
And hopeful.
And when I lose it.
You help me find it.
I am a hope-bearer.
You are the hope I share.
Christ, be with me. May I be a hope-bearer.
Christ, be with me.
Amen.

24. HEAL

Christ, be with me. Life is crashing down around me. Christ, be with me.

I AM A PERSON OF FAITH. A CHRISTIAN. AN EPISCOPALIAN. SO MUCH of my worldview is colored by the lenses of my faith background. But this book is not written only for people who consider themselves Christian. This book is written for anyone who needs it.

Still, a significant source of encouragement and support for me is the Bible. Particularly the stories of Jesus's interaction with people like you and me. Stories that pull me in are those about people who long for healing, whether from a physical or soul illness. Stories about mental and spiritual struggles.

We know the stories. Like the one about the woman who touched Jesus in his robe and was healed. Or the story of the man whose vision was restored when Jesus took mud and spit and rubbed it on his eyes. There are even moments when Jesus speaks life, and death is vanquished. These stories of healing are dramatic, newsworthy, and shocking.

There are faith traditions where healing features dramatic physical healing—laying on of hands, anointing with oil, and emotional testimonies. These traditions are faithful and have deep roots in the practice of healing. I do not come out of that tradition, even though there have certainly been moments when I wish I did. But I don't.

Healing looks different to everyone.

I work across the street from Houston's Texas Medical Center, the largest hospital in the nation. The church where I serve welcomes, each week, medical center staff, caregivers, and patients receiving care. Look out across our congregation, and you will see bald heads and hospital bracelets. And you'll see tears of fear, gratitude, and exhaustion. Being in the presence of these guests is a profound honor.

Most Sunday mornings you can find me sitting at the "Welcome Tent" set up in front of the church, and I'll sometimes meet someone who found us by simply walking by. In 2022, a gentleman happened to stroll in. I saw this man as he exited the building following the service. If grief, fear, and feeling overwhelmed had a face, it would be his.

Those of us in the tent knew he was carrying something heavy. The dam built up inside him broke with our gentle invitation and hospitality. It was apparent to me that the tears that fell from his eyes had needed to be released for some time.

His beloved was fighting for her life. Cancer, the monster that it is, had found its way into the area around her heart, preventing the doctors from treating the damage occurring to her most vital organ.

As he shared his story with us, his grief and devastation remained, but I began to see a lifting of his spirit. With wet cheeks, he said he experienced a bit of healing that day and felt intense gratitude. He talked about the sermon. He spoke of how the music lifted his weary soul. He asked us to pray for him and for his wife.

We did, and we do.

I share the story with you because healing is often presented as cut and dried. You are healed, or you're not. You are fixed, or you're broken.

I've learned during my journey with mental illness that healing is multifaceted and doesn't always look like what we expect it to. I can't heal my anxiety or your anxiety and will always be wary of those who claim they can.

Personally, I find it much more helpful to approach the idea of healing when I encounter the holy. Moments of grace. Moments when I notice my breath is regulated. Moments of interaction with a piece of music or work of visual art.

The gentleman I met in church experienced healing by being in a place that honored and welcomed his tears. He experienced healing when telling his love story. He experienced healing when he trusted his gut enough to sit in the church with others. Maybe it was his gut, but I think it might be more than that.

Healing looks different for everyone.

Living so close to the Texas Medical Center has taught me that healing takes shape in ways that we long pray it wouldn't. Occasionally, I learn of someone who has died after an illness. The family says they prayed for healing, and their loved one has healed. Not in the way they had hoped, but in time, they recognize that the end of the pain and suffering of their loved one is a form of healing.

My anxiety has not healed—it is sometimes managed. And, with the help of a loving family, supportive community, caring medical professionals, medication, and the implementation of countless strategies and exercises—much of which I've included in this book—that anxiety is managed more often than not.

You are not alone in your healing journey. It may feel like it at times, but you're not alone. I know this because, even though I might not know you personally, I am making space for you in my prayers, actions, and how I express gratitude for this life I have been given.

I began this chapter by highlighting the stories of Jesus, particularly the stories where he heals those who need it. And now, I see those stories with new eyes.

Maybe healing is not a single occurrence but a moment in time that sends ripples into the world that washes over each of us.

INVITATION

You are a miracle.

I could have you write this over and over one hundred times, but I will not do that. Instead, I invite you to reflect on what it means to be a miracle.

Maybe you create a work of art, a dance, a poem, or a song. Maybe you go for a walk and take note of the miracles surrounding you. Maybe you sit in front of a mirror and speak these words to yourself.

You are a miracle.

You are a miracle.

You are a miracle.

REFLECTION

- How has your life been impacted by miracles?
- Do you believe in miracles? Why or why not?

SUPPLICATION

Christ, be with me. Life is crashing down around me.
Christ, be with me.

It feels like everything is crashing down around me.

Life hurts and I am tired of hurting.

I'm behind at work.

My relationships are suffering.

All I want to do is sleep.

I want to hide.

I want to give up.

My life is crashing down around me

But I am not alone.

I am never alone.

I am never alone.
Those words sound empty.
Help me to know that you are with me in the crashing.
You are with me in the picking up the pieces.
Christ, be with me. Life is crashing down around me.
Christ, be with me.
Amen.

25. Giving

Christ, be with me in my giving and receiving. Christ, be with me.

I HAVE CHAMPAGNE TASTE ON A BEER BUDGET. I LOVE NICE THINGS. I enjoy quality and high-level design.

And that, my friends, can impact one's financial bottom line.

I also find great joy in giving gifts to people. Birthday gifts, Christmas gifts, and just-because gifts. The occasion doesn't matter! The older and deeper into the publishing world I've gotten, the more I love giving children's picture books as gifts. And people seem to love receiving them. Receiving a well-written, well-designed picture book isn't much different from receiving a personalized work of art.

Children's books are also wonderful gifts and resources for adults. A few years ago, a team of parents, including my wife and me, facilitated a parenting class—even though it is notoriously difficult to find a good curriculum in the space. Either it's too biblical or not enough. Too heavy-handed or not enough. Too conservative or too liberal.

So, we came up with a creative plan: no curriculum, good coffee, and picture books.

Each week a different person would read a children's book to the group and facilitate a conversation on the themes of the picture book they shared. You name a theme, and we covered it. We discussed sex, politics, parenting styles, neurodiversity, eating habits, sleeping habits, emotions, communication, grief, death, divorce, sibling relationships, learning difficulties, family systems, humor, school challenges, body image, diversity, racism, classism, and more.

All of this is from children's books!

We learned a lot from the picture books but possibly even more from the group's hilarious and sometimes challenging conversations. And once we finished with a book, we'd donate it to the children's library at our church.

The topic of this chapter is "gift." The truth is, I really wanted to focus on the importance of giving yourself a gift.

If you are engaging at all with your anxiety, making healthy choices like building silence into your life, or setting realistic goals, then you deserve to treat yourself to something special.

We are nearing the end of our time together, and I am hopeful that you feel the encouragement and support I'm trying to send you through these words in pages.

When I began writing this book, I decided to mark the accomplishment with two gifts. I deeply admire the mid-century-modern aesthetic, particularly items designed by Charles and Ray Eames. I have always wanted a pair of the Eames Plywood Lounge Chairs. I researched, looked high and low, and found a perfect pair of Eames LCW chairs for my office.

They make me happy and are the perfect gift for me—especially as I began to understand the depth and breadth of work I put into myself, my mental and physical health, and this writing project.

INVITATION

You are invited to go to the library or a bookstore and choose a few picture books that spark your interest and read them.

Read them once—then reread them. Finally, choose a phrase or illustration from the book that speaks to you. Maybe it is a children's book on grief or friendship, or maybe it's a book that makes you laugh. Honor the child within—and see what happens!

REFLECTION

- What gift are you going to treat yourself with?
- What did you learn from the picture books you selected?

SUPPLICATION

Christ, be with me in my giving and receiving.
Christ, be with me.
Help me to give myself to others.
But not too much.
Help me to share my heart.
But not too much.
Help me to walk with others.
And help me to know when I don't have the strength.
I am a giver.
I always have been.
I enjoy giving gifts.
I like the smiles and the warmth of hugs.
It is more difficult for me to receive.
Praise makes me uncomfortable.
Criticism cuts me to my soul.
Help me to be a giver.
And receiver.
Christ, be with me in my giving and receiving.
Christ, be with me.
Amen.

26. Color

Christ, be with me in the colors that surround me. Christ, be with me.

I CAN'T WRITE A BOOK ABOUT ANXIETY AND FEAR WITHOUT TALKING about color or remembering when my heart found its calling.

My earliest memories are filled with color. The fragrant red of a garden-grown tomato. The towering green pines that surrounded my childhood. The deep blue of the Louisiana sky. The chattering song of my pappaw's purple martins. Stained-glass windows spilling puddles of radiant jewel tones across the church floor.

The connection we have with color is nearly impossible to describe with words.

- *Color tells a story.*
- *Color helps us to remember.*
- *Color inspires us to dream.*
- *Color provides hope.*
- *Color walks with us as we grieve.*
- *Color is all around us.*
- *Color is our song.*
- *Color gives life to our anger.*
- *Color fights for justice.*
- *Color helps us to pray.*

Now more than ever, color teaches us to love our neighbor.

My first book, *The Painting Table: A Journey of Loss and Joy,* brought inspiration to conduct Painting Table workshops and eventually connected me with the Sandy Hook Elementary community, where I worked with those impacted by the December 14, 2012, school shooting.

It was a beautiful Friday morning, my day off. I will, on occasion, spend my Fridays painting with children in local schools. Hammond School in Columbia, South Carolina, had invited me to paint with children in their Lower School. They were studying about the continent of Africa and wanted me to work with them on a style of painting called "Tinga Tinga," which developed in the second half of the twentieth century in Tanzania and later spread to most of East Africa. These days there are various Tinga Tinga schools of painting—from intricate and detailed animals intertwined with the feathers of peacocks, to tourist-oriented work with simple stylized characters at the base of Mt. Kilimanjaro. The colors are almost always intense and bright.

That Friday morning we painted and learned together. We "traveled" to Tanzania. There were bold colors and lots of laughter. The joy of childhood was palpable.

Little did I know that at that same time I was working with school children in Columbia, South Carolina, sheer terror and tragedy was unfolding in the hallways and classrooms of a small-town elementary school in a community called Sandy Hook.

What happened on December 14, 2012, brought the world to its knees.

Three months later, I was contacted about bringing a Painting Table session to Newtown. The director of Christian education at Trinity Episcopal Church in Newtown was looking for ways to gather the children to talk about faith and God and what happened. Trinity Church, Newtown is a congregation that serves many families with children who attended Sandy Hook Elementary. Ben Wheeler, a child of the congregation, was one of the children killed.

With tears in my eyes and an anxious heart, I said "yes."

On Friday, May 3, we pulled into Newtown . . . and I fell in love.

Again, it was a gorgeous day. The skies were a clear crystal blue. The temperature was hovering around 70 degrees. The rolling green hills were dotted with yellow forsythia and pink cherry blossoms. An American flag waved proudly in the center of town. And kids were everywhere because class let out early that day.

Once we arrived at the church, we prepared the undercroft for the Painting Table workshop. We had arranged to have two sessions—one for children and families, and one for adults only. We expected that there might be twenty or so people who participated, but when it was all said and done, over fifty children and adults joined in.

The room was set up with round tables. On each table we had canvas paper, paints, baby wipes, toothpicks, cotton swabs, pencils, writing paper, and scraps of cardboard. Everyone gathered at the tables—mothers with their children, friend with friend, and neighbor with neighbor. We lit a candle, I gave a few instructions, and the painting began.

That day was one I'll never forget. We were especially thrilled to have Ana Hernandez join us. Ana is a composer, arranger, and performer of sacred music. She brought a number of different instruments and her music filled the space. Peoples' conversations were not overwhelmed but held aloft. When the children were finished painting (and hands were washed!), Ana invited them to play with the different instruments. It was a joyful sound!

The end result of the Painting Table workshop is not the painting that is created. It is the conversation, sharing, and listening that takes place around the table. It is one mother comforting another mother as they both grieve for their friend who lost a child. It is about the conversation I had with a third-grade girl who told me she had had a really bad day. Her painting was dark and frantic. I listened to her for a little while—then encouraged her to paint another one. The second painting was a bit more colorful. She took her two paintings and smashed them together. When she pulled them apart, the darkness had lifted. I could see light and love . . . and a beautiful smile.

The Painting Table is also about the conversation I had with a young mother who told me that she feels guilty sometimes that she still has her children. She shared with me what it was like to take her children home on that tragic day—passing house after house with state patrol cars in the driveways.

Or the mother who told me how her first-grader, a big boy for his age, had climbed up into her lap and sobbed when he learned that his friend was not going to be there when he returned to school.

I am hopeful that sharing these stories brought some sort of peace to their lives. There will always be twenty-six holes in the hearts of these people and their community. I also believe that within the grief that exists, there is much healing and possibility.

While there is grief, sadness, and loss, there is also hope. There is an opportunity for celebration as we gather together, break bread, talk, and are welcomed. Whether it is through cooking, painting, or Eucharist, we come together to remember.

There is a subtle rhythm to what happens when people gather around the Painting Table. Participants are often guarded, and I sense a palpable fear in the air—the familiar one of "I'm not 'good' enough. I'm not an artist." Participants will sit for a moment staring at the blank paper. They ask me what they should paint, and I encourage them to tell their own story using color, not words.

In time, the room's rhythm and "air" begin to change. Fingers are dipped into the paint, and stories form on paper or canvas.

Bodies relax, and fingers dance a new creation across the surface of the page. It's beautiful, really.

The conversation around the table also comes in waves. People are working on their own projects, but they know they are part of a larger community. There is talking followed by silence. I do not guide this. It happens on its own. Often, the rhythm of the group reminds me of breathing.

Gathering around the Painting Table is Eucharistic in nature. There is a connection to something more profound. It is a glimpse into our souls. For some, the experience can only be described as holy. People begin to relax; for many, it is the first time they have settled in days or weeks. Frequently there are tears. There are always gentle smiles.

I once led a session where a young mother of two children, ages two and eight-and-a-half months, painted a beautiful angel. But unfortunately, the angel was her husband. He had died suddenly just one month earlier. He was only thirty years old. Painting gave her the space to grieve. It helped her to remember that her husband would always be with her and their children.[1]

I currently serve as the director of Christian formation and parish life at Palmer Memorial Episcopal Church in Houston, Texas. Archway Academy, one of the largest sober high schools in the country, is located on Palmer's campus. This high school is made up of young people who are fighting every day to live and is run by adults who have walked similar journeys. Sometimes, the students make poor decisions and one of the teachers or a member of the administration will call me to let me know that there is a student who would like to speak to me.

Even though it's challenging to not know what they want to talk about in advance, I always say "yes" and have never regretted the experience. While every meeting has been profound in its own way, there are two specific stories I'd like to share.

One afternoon, while I'm sitting in my office, talking with my colleague and friend Ryan, Archway's director comes to my door with two students in tow. She asks if we have a few minutes to talk to these students. Of course, we did.

I instantly assumed that the students were found in a closet or an empty classroom, doing *something* they shouldn't be doing. Before they even sat down, I was trying to formulate my response. Maybe that is why my wife gave me a coaster that says, "Talk less. Listen more." I'm no prude, and I have the sense of humor of a thirteen-year-old, so I was willing myself not to giggle.

The director invited them to speak.

The young man, obviously nervous, but also a bit smug, began sharing. And what he shared was completely unexpected.

He wanted me to know that they had gotten caught for . . . wait for it . . . dispensing fart spray in the hallways of the school. As you can imagine, the giggle button inside of me was pushed, and I almost lost it.

You would be proud to know that I held it together.

I looked over at Ryan, and she, too, was working hard to keep a straight face.

I wasn't exactly sure what the director wanted us to say to the students, so I told them that I respected the daily struggle they faced related to their addiction. I also told them that while I appreciate the healing power of humor, play, and silliness, there is an appropriate time and place for those kinds of releases, and maybe the hallways at a school, in a church, on a day when we were having a funeral, might not be the best time to fill the hallways with fart spray.

Everyone was nodding, and I could have stopped there. But I didn't. I had to know where they bought the fart spray. I needed some! The young woman couldn't believe that I asked and was more than excited to tell me. Later that day, I may or may not have gone and purchased my own.

The second story begins in a similar way.

"I have a student that I would like to speak with you."

I, of course, invited them to stop in my office.

With permission, the director wanted me to know that this young woman had recently had a breakthrough in therapy and felt ready to share her writing and journal entries with her therapist. Then with the director of the school. And now, this young woman was willing to explore her writing with me. She didn't know me from Adam, so kudos for her bravery.

She agreed to do so, opened her tattered and much beloved journal, and began reading to me. As this deeply wounded and profoundly powerful young woman began reading her words, I was transported and transfixed. Her use of language, sparse and perfectly placed, created some of the most powerful writing I have ever come across.

There was a poem about a young woman, fighting for her life, navigating addiction, abuse by men, and a palpable desire to not only live, but to change the world. I didn't just want to sit there with my chin on my desk, drooling over the perfection of her prose, so I thought of some constructive feedback.

I encouraged her to slow down when she was reading. That felt like safe constructive criticism. We talked about cadence and rhythm. We talked about rhyme and the importance of each word she puts on the page. I encouraged her to keep writing, and I offered to be her guinea pig if she ever wanted to bounce her new work off me.

In the gifting of her words, her pain, and her dreams with her therapist, the director of the school, and with me, this young woman was breaking out of a prison she had been in for most of her life. When she entered my office, I could see in her body language that she was nervous and afraid. Her shoulders were hunched over, and her head was turned down. As she departed my office, she appeared to be taller and lighter. There was a sparkle in her eyes and color in her smile. She thanked me and disappeared down the hall.

I share these two stories because they have everything to do with color.

When we experience play, humor, and yes, naughty fun, like running through your school with fart spray, or waves of release and healing when our imprisoned souls break free, our voice is heard, and our collective world fills with color.

People are desperate for connection, color, and hope. We live in a world where fear of the "other" threatens to take hold.

We can't let that happen.

———————

It is late afternoon in France under a crisp blue sky. A volunteer in the open-air kitchen, I am covered from head to toe in water and soap bubbles. The sea of voices around me rises like a symphony, instruments that I do not recognize, yet long to understand and know. I hear sounds of laughter and joy. So much unrestrained laughter and joy.

There are faces that I recognize. I see a young woman and a young man who traveled with me to Taize: Tom saw God's face clearly for the first time as he looked into the painted face of the crucified Jesus icon in the community church. Hillary feels in her heart that she will never be the same person she was before this journey. She, too, saw God's face. Then, there are faces that I do not know, but have seen before.

When I was young, I used to pore over my grandmother's copies of *National Geographic* magazine. I would look for hours at the pictures of the strikingly beautiful African men and women. As I gaze across the way, I see them again.

It is as if the picture in the magazine has come to life.

That beautiful black face. Those dark and deep eyes. The bright, encompassing smile. Then I glance across to the faces of my new friends, Adrian and Olgutsa. A boyfriend and girlfriend who traveled to this small village from Romania are also seeking the face of God. They too communicate with laughter, broken English, and their eyes.

No longer separated by the water of the ocean, we communicate over a basin of dishwater. This is a more honest and sincere form of conversation than I have ever experienced. It is not with our voices, for we speak different languages. It is with our eyes, and it is with our laughter. We are speaking the colorful language of the heart. And we are washing dishes.

I look down into the basin of dishwater and at the reflection of the faces of my new friends. The dancing water and the shifting light have caused our faces to become one. My deepest longing is that we continue to gather around the table and share the holy bread of peace and love with each other. It might be with paints, and it might be with words. It might be washing dishes.[2]

Whatever shape it takes, we need to make space for it to happen.

INVITATION

You are invited to stretch this exercise out over the next week or month.

I would like for you to use your phone's camera or other camera to take color-specific photographs on your daily walk around your home or where you work. Pick seven different colors and divide them up over the week or over the month.

Monday might be the day you look for blue things. Tuesday might be orange, and so on. This exercise will help you notice the colors that surround you. Colors we often miss.

Once you've collected those images, I invite you to write about them in your journal.

This is a remarkable exercise that shows you just how much we miss as we move through life.

REFLECTION

- What colors did you choose and why?
- What, if anything, did you learn about yourself through this exercise?
- How will you apply what you learned moving forward?

SUPPLICATION

Christ, be with me in the colors that surround me.
Christ, be with me.
There are colors all around.
But I fail to see them
I miss the bluebird.
I ignore the yellow sunflower.
Busyness colors my world.
Anxiety fogs my vision.
Help me to see the green of new life.
Help me to see the silence of a gray sky in winter.
The orange of a campfire's flickering flame.
And help me never forget that those I've loved and lost
remain in the colors that surround me.
Christ, be with me in the colors that surround me.
Christ, be with me
Amen.

27. Awe

Christ, be with me in moments of awe and wonder. Christ, be with me.

WE ALL HAVE THOSE MOMENTS WHEN WE LOOK UP AT THE STARS ON A dark night or gaze out of the window of an airplane and experience the awareness of just how tiny we are. I remember the first time I went camping in a location where there was very little light pollution. The night sky was as dark as I had ever seen it.

I was a camp counselor at Camp Kanuga in Hendersonville, North Carolina. For many of the boys in my cabin, this was the first time they had ever camped out, much less in a place with the darkness so palpable.

One of my favorite memories is sitting with these little guys and looking up at the stars. Someone would point out a planet, some sort of space shuttle or satellite, or even a shooting star, and this wave of excitement would shoot through the group. Not unlike the star itself.

What I remember the most from those nights is the sense of wonder and the awareness of our place in creation. The awareness that even though we are tiny, we are part of something incredible.

I also remember the first time I flew in an airplane.

As a child, I lived with my head in the clouds. I was a daydreamer and a thinker. I also had undiagnosed ADHD. But this was the first time I was "for real" in the clouds. I could see teeny tiny houses and teeny tiny swimming pools. I felt so small. I also began to understand the importance of the decisions we make.

When I experienced my mental health crisis, my anxiety proudly took its perceived position in the center of the universe and proclaimed the following:

"Your fears are the worst."

"Your struggles are the worst."

"You are a terrible human being."

"You are the reason why this project is going to fail."

"You are a terrible writer."

"No one is going to read your book."

"This is ego, yes."

"It is also anxiety telling another lie."

The liar is telling you that you are not worth anything.

"You are crazy."

"You are broken."

———————

I have a substantial commute to work. It takes me thirty minutes to an hour most days, twice a day. But I cherish this time. I enjoy listening to podcasts. I also enjoy looking at people in the cars next to me. Not because I am a stalker, but because I like imagining their story.

The trouble comes when they catch me looking at them. That's when I do a quick head nod or "good old boy" greeting—you know the one. You lift your finger off the steering wheel acknowledging that they saw you—the famous pickup truck wave.

My point in telling you the story about the stars, the story about the airplane, and the story about the commute is because each of these stories reminds me that I'm but a grain of sand or twinkling star in the whole of creation.

Our lives may seem small when looking at the stars or down through the clouds from an airplane, and when we are in those places of panic and anxiety, our fears and worries take over. It feels like they are going to choke the life out of us. Anxiety tells us that if we fail a test, then our lives are over.

In taking the time to get outside, we can hit reboot and experience moments of awe that help us to see that our fears and worries have no power. By grounding ourselves in moments of awe and wonder, we break the cycle of anxiety. The worries don't disappear, but they are put in their place.

Photography and walking outdoors has saved my life. I can go for a walk, look for birds, observe the colors of the leaves on the ground or the shapes of the clouds in the sky, and my anxiety settles.

My life is awe-full. Not awful. How crazy is it that the removal of two letters can change the meaning of the word so significantly?

Now go forth and lead your awe-full life.

INVITATION

You are invited to reflect on the places where you have experienced feelings of awe.

Maybe it is gazing out across the ocean. Maybe it is on a mountaintop. Or the delivery room. Maybe it is in your lover's arms. Maybe it is in a moment of silence, or while listening to your favorite song.

Open yourself to these moments of awe.

REFLECTION

- How does it feel when you are experiencing moments of awe?
- Describe, in detail, a time when you caught your breath and experienced an overwhelming sense of wonder.
- How can you open yourself up to more of these moments?

SUPPLICATION

Christ, be with me in moments of awe and wonder.
Christ, be with me.
My breath quickens.
My eyes widen.
My heart breaks open.
I find strength and rootedness on the holy ground of awe and
wonder.
Help me to open myself to wonder.
Help me to seek and share moments of awe.
Help me learn from children I know and love.
Childhood wonder.
Childhood excitement.
Help me to ask questions and learn more.
Help me to see what is right in front of me.
Christ, be with me in moments of awe and wonder.
Christ, be with me.
Amen.

28. RITUAL

Christ, be with me in the rituals of my daily life. Christ, be with me.

YOUR STORY WILL CERTAINLY LOOK DIFFERENT FROM MINE, BUT I BET there is commonality in the feelings we still carry. I experienced my parents' divorce, financial instability, illness, and so much more. As I reflected on my origin story, I did not realize just how much it impacted me. This is not to beat up on my parents. They loved us. Cared for us and did all they could for us. They still do.

But it is important to me that I unmask my childhood. When my divorced mom fell head over heels in love with the local Episcopal priest, and they eventually married, life changed significantly.

We began experiencing new rituals. Your assumption might be that I am referring to the rituals of the church. Yes, that is part of it, but I'm talking more about the rituals that took place in our home. Rituals we had never experienced. Papa, as we call him, introduced our family to end-of-the-day tea parties.

When Papa was in seminary, he had a friend from China, and they would have late night tea parties. This was not the kind of tea party where you get dressed up and invite guests, but an intentional and peaceful way to end the day.

Papa introduced that into our home. We used beautiful pottery from China. We learned about different loose-leaf teas. I was shocked to learn that loose-leaf tea does not come prepackaged in tea bags and, as such, keeps its flavor, aroma, and health benefits. Until then, I only knew of Lipton tea bags. I thought we were fancy-pants when we practiced the ritual, which was as ancient as time itself.

I also learned about steeping balls, infusers, French presses, and strainers. My world broke wide open!

We sat on the floor around a low table. The tea would steep. The aroma danced in the air around us. We talked about our day. We were able to catch our breaths. It was a ritual that brought a deep peace and calm into the stressful life of a preteen who was longing for something to keep him afloat. We shared little cookies and various teas.

As I got older and more engaged in the rituals of the Episcopal Church, I fell hard for the Order of Compline, an ancient prayer service that is prayed at the conclusion of every day.

There is a gentle rhythm that prepares my soul for rest. For someone who has sensory issues, it is a gentle and inclusive way to pray. It is grounding, calm, and peaceful. It is ritual and a rhythm.

Often, I turn to the service when I can't sleep or when I am afraid. It was where I turned in the middle of the night while my family was hunkered down in closets during the onslaught of Hurricane Harvey, particularly the first night when tornadoes were touching down all around us. I repeated the words over and over and over. They were a lifeboat for me.

Below are some of my favorite passages, prayers, and responses from The Order of Compline, which can be found on page 127 in the Book of Common Prayer.

"The Lord Almighty grant us a peaceful night and a perfect end. *Amen.*"

Psalm 91 *Qui habitat*

[1] He who dwells in the shelter of the Most High *
abides under the shadow of the Almighty.

2 He shall say to the Lord,
"You are my refuge and my stronghold, *
my God in whom I put my trust."
3 He shall deliver you from the snare of the hunter *
and from the deadly pestilence.
4 He shall cover you with his pinions,
and you shall find refuge under his wings; *
his faithfulness shall be a shield and buckler.
5 You shall not be afraid of any terror by night, *
nor of the arrow that flies by day;
6 Of the plague that stalks in the darkness, *
nor of the sickness that lays waste at mid-day.
7 A thousand shall fall at your side
and ten thousand at your right hand, *
but it shall not come near you.
8 Your eyes have only to behold *
to see the reward of the wicked.
9 Because you have made the Lord your refuge, *
and the Most High your habitation,
10 There shall no evil happen to you, *
neither shall any plague come near your dwelling.
11 For he shall give his angels charge over you, *
to keep you in all your ways.
12 They shall bear you in their hands, *
lest you dash your foot against a stone.
13 You shall tread upon the lion and the adder; *
you shall trample the young lion and the serpent
under your feet.
14 Because he is bound to me in love,
therefore will I deliver him; *
I will protect him, because he knows my Name.

Come to me, all who labor and are heavy-laden, and I will
give you rest. Take my yoke upon you and learn from me;
for I am gentle and lowly in heart, and you will find rest for
your souls. For my yoke is easy, and my burden is light.
Matthew 11:28–30

Keep watch, dear Lord, with those who work, or watch, or
weep this night, and give your angels charge over those who
sleep. Tend the sick, Lord Christ; give rest to the weary, bless
the dying, soothe the suffering, pity the afflicted, shield the
joyous; and all for your love's sake. *Amen.*

Guide us waking, O Lord, and guard us sleeping; that awake
we may watch with Christ, and asleep we may rest in peace.

Lord, you now have set your servant free *
  to go in peace as you have promised;
For these eyes of mine have seen the Savior, *
  whom you have prepared for all the world to see:
A Light to enlighten the nations, *
  and the glory of your people Israel.
Glory to the Father, and to the Son, and to the Holy Spirit: *
  as it was in the beginning, is now, and will be forever. Amen.

. . . and we repeat the Antiphon:
    Guide us waking, O Lord, and guard us sleeping; that
awake we may watch with Christ, and asleep we may rest
in peace.[1]

What I have learned from this, and why I share this idea with
you, is because we live in anxious times. There is instability and
fear. We are unmoored.

We must reintroduce ritual into our lives. Maybe it is what you do in the evening to prepare yourself for a night of rest. Maybe it is making your bed in the morning before you leave for the day. Maybe it is how you eat a meal. Maybe it's a daily walk outdoors or on a treadmill. Maybe it is a nap on Sunday afternoon.

Slow down. Notice the colors. The taste. The texture. The aroma.

I remember so clearly looking forward to having teatime with my family. Until I sat down to write this book, I had forgotten about that time in my life. I had forgotten about that ritual.

My daily ritual now involves charging my literal camera batteries before I go to bed to charge my own batteries. When I wake up, I take a cold shower, eat a high-protein, low carb breakfast, and then head to our neighborhood park. Once there, I will greet a friend or two and begin my walk through the woods.

People often call me the bird whisperer, and there is some truth to that. When I am walking on the trail and in the zone, my senses are heightened. Particularly my hearing and my eyes. It seems like the birds know me—or at least know that I am one of the good guys.

I know this might sound silly. That is not my intention. I am learning how to live and thrive from these amazing creatures. I am learning to find my song in morning and focus on what gives me strength. I'm learning how to spread my wings and fly.

Excuse me, I am going to have teatime.

You are welcome to join me.

INVITATION

You are invited to reflect on the different rituals in your life.

When I began to examine my own rituals, I discovered that I had forgotten so many of the rituals that gave me life. It was in the rediscovery of these lost rituals, and implementation of new ones, I found the center of my soul.

I found me.

REFLECTION

- What are some of your daily rituals? What about seasonal rituals?
- How does participating in these rituals bring peace? If they don't bring peace, how might you change them around or introduce a new ritual?

SUPPLICATION

Christ, be with me in the rituals of my daily life.
Christ, be with me.
Wake.
Give thanks.
Greet a loved one.
Maybe it is my reflection I greet with love.
Prepare a meal.
Listen for the song of a sparrow on the wind.
Light a candle.
Stretch and grow.
Help me to recognize the rituals in my life.
Help me to keep what is helpful.
Help me release what is not.
Christ, be with me in the rituals of my daily life.
Christ, be with me.
Amen.

29. Purpose

Christ, be with me as I seek to find my purpose. Christ, be with me.

THE QUESTION BEGINS BEFORE WE EVEN KNOW HOW TO READ OR count. We were asked and we ask our children, "What do you want to be when you grow up?"

I never realized what a ridiculous question this is, especially for the littlest ones in our midst. Maybe there is a better way to pose the question. What do you enjoy? What makes you happy? What gives you energy? What makes you laugh? What makes you feel strong? What makes you, you?

What if we ask these questions instead?

This is also an incredibly difficult question to answer for young people in high school or college, when so many changes are happening all at once—socially, physically, relationally, spiritually, and in countless other ways.

The pressure that these young people are going through is crushing, especially now. The political atmosphere in this country is choking us to death. Suicide rates are skyrocketing. The crisis of unchecked or unmanaged mental illness often leads to addiction, self-harm, destructive relationships, isolation, and so much more.

How amazing would it be if we started our schooling with required formational opportunities focusing on play, mental wellness, age-appropriate questions and struggles, and resources for understanding our emotions and navigating our emotional landscape. And because we don't have something like this, you can look around at just about any adult, including the adult you see in the mirror, and see someone who is hurting, struggling, or searching.

What does it really mean to grow up? Does it mean being an adult? Does it mean paying bills? Does it mean having a family or paying for health insurance?

If that's the case, being a grown-up doesn't sound like much fun. And I find that sad.

The first time I heard the word "call" in relationship to "what is God calling you into" was when I became a part of the Episcopal Church. The assumption seems to be that "call" means going to seminary. "Call" can mean any number of things—going to college, becoming a teacher, a doctor, or a lawyer. Maybe it means becoming a welder, an artist, or a poet.

The first time I heard the word "avocation," I remember thinking it was a word I really liked. Your vocation is what you do for a job. Your avocation is something you do for fun, maybe as a hobby, or creative outlet. I don't know why vocation and avocation must live in separate houses.

I've reached a point in my life where my vocation and avocation are roommates. While I feel very lucky that my vocation is, in a way, also my avocation, that balance has taken me a lifetime to figure out.

This is a long game, and the scary question comes in those moments of self-reflection or self-degradation when comparing yourself to others. And you begin wondering what your purpose in life is. This is a question that could easily take you into an anxious place. On the other hand, it can be fun to explore. Ask the kinds of questions I shared earlier—the alternative questions to "What do you want to be when you grow up?"

I have learned that my anxiety, stress, and worry ease when I have a purpose. I'm not talking about the big-purpose-in-life question. I'm talking about the hour-by-hour, day-to-day goals and decisions you make that give your life meaning. It's the kind of thing that enables you to get out of your head. Maybe it is something as simple as serving your neighbor or participating in a spontaneous moment of fun and laughter.

When we focus on the big questions, especially those of us with a tendency to worry, we can get lost and overwhelmed. It is much easier to see and explore what our purpose is when we approach our lives with love and grace.

Be kind to yourself.

Come to think of it, I still don't know what I want to be when I grow up, and that suits me just fine.

INVITATION

You are invited to explore what it means to live a purposeful life.

I recently learned of the Japanese concept of Ikigai:

Ikigai lies in the realm of community, family, friendships and in the roles you fulfill. When you pursue your ikigai, you are not out to save the world. It is more about connecting with and helping the people who give meaning to your life—your family, friends, co-workers and community. You don't have to be good at something to find your ikigai. Ikigai can be a very simple practice, a daily ritual or the practice of a new hobby. Ikigai is more about growth rather than mastery. It is not a destination or goal to achieve. It does encompass goals, but with ikigai there is no destination. Ikigai is not about what you want out of life. Ikigai is about who you want to become—your actualized self. Ikigai is future-oriented and long-term and, as such, involves the pursuit of goals. As goals are personal, meaningful and involve effort and persistence, the pursuit of them can lead to a sense of well-being. And goals give us a sense of purpose, thus pursuing them makes life worth living.

An important point to make about goals in relation to ikigai is the achievement of them is not as important as the process and effort that goes into them.[1]

REFLECTION

- What are your core values?
- What beliefs are important to you?
- What is your role in your family, workplace, and the local community?
- What relationships are important to you and define who you are?
- What are your hobbies and interests?
- What things would you like to learn or try?
- When are you most present?

SUPPLICATION

Christ, be with me as I seek to find my purpose.
Christ, be with me.
As I explore:
My passions.
My place in the world.
The power of my voice.
The joy of my heart.
The service of my hands.
The journey of my feet.
The reach of my arms.
The depth of my soul.
The wisdom of my head.

The beginning is near.
Christ, be with me as I seek to find my purpose.
Christ, be with me.
Amen.

30. CONNECTION

Christ, be with me as I strive for connection. Christ, be with me.

UNTIL QUARANTINE HAPPENED, I DON'T THINK I TRULY UNDERSTOOD what connection, or lack thereof, truly meant. We all know what happened. The week began, and life was normal. By the end of that week, all our lives were forever changed.

We were told to order groceries. We were told not to gather in groups. We were told not to go to school. We were told not to go to work. We were told not to go to church or synagogue or temple. We were told we could die, and countless people did. We watched in horror as the national and international media showed just how terrifying, deadly, and relentless this virus could be. We were also told it wasn't real, that it was a "deep fake" creation by the liberals.

Infectious disease specialists were doing their very best to provide us with timely information and best practices for navigating a hell we have never experienced before. Other leaders made light of the virus and called it a joke. Not only were we disconnected from the rituals and gatherings of our normal lives, but our country also became more and more disconnected.

That disconnection continues.

For a while, the privileged and lucky among us fell into a rhythm that felt somewhat like a vacation. Then it became a hassle. And soon enough, it became a crisis of disconnection, social withdrawal, and loneliness. We still do not know how it will all play out. A microscopic entity has changed the trajectory for so many and for our world.

I remember when our church was given approval from medical professionals at the national level and local level to be able to gather for worship outdoors. Up early, and before just about anyone else arrived, I would head over to our outdoor green space, walk eight feet, put a stake flag in the ground, walk another eight feet, put another flag in the ground, walk another eight feet, and put another flag in the ground.

I averaged about seventy flags.

This was my Sunday morning ritual—week after week after week. Households were asked to bring their own chairs and sit in the space near a flag, leaving a minimum of six feet between them and the next household. It was hopeful and devastating—all at the same time.

You could see the pain and struggle in the eyes of your community. Disconnection and weariness replaced connection and hope.

Much of my childhood was spent feeling lonely, and it continues to impact how I move through life. Relationships and friendships carry significant importance to me. That's why it hurts so much when relationships become toxic or hurtful.

Quarantine opened my eyes to how important connection was to me. I especially missed my connection to Palmer Memorial Episcopal Church. We are just like any family. There's a gossipy aunt, the grumpy grandfather, the dramatic sibling, and the center of attention matriarch. There's pouting, hurt feelings, the occasional runaway, and the prodigal son. We can be ugly to each other and love each other at the same time. Then there are the times we gather and hold each other up as hearts break and tears fall.

As you well know, photography gave me a sense of connection to the world that I was missing. On one of my earlier walks during Covid time, I took photographs of chains and locks. My therapist could have a field day with this, but it was a helpful meditation for me.

What was I chained to? What was I locked out of, or locked into? When looking at the links of the chain, I wondered who I was connected to. A chain is not a chain without each individual link. At the time, I was feeling like a single link with little connection to others. I also reflected on the key that would unlock the locks. And I wondered who was holding the key?

Maybe this is a bunch of hoo-hah and you're wondering if I'm a bit off my rocker. And maybe I am! But it is in moments like these, when you focus or meditate on an idea or experience like connection and disconnection, that you learn more about your heart and soul.

I posted the lock and chain photos on Facebook, thinking my followers would ignore them. I was surprised when I received many comments and lengthy reflections on what these images meant to people.

These photos gave shape to an experience that we all were feeling.

Before we move on to the final reflection of this book, I want to tell you the story of my garage, where I ended up working during Covid. My wife, a schoolteacher, set up office in our dining room. I set up my office in the garage.

I opened the garage each morning and sat at my table and worked. I hung a beautiful tapestry behind me, so you'd see that and not our washer and dryer during my countless Zoom calls. I filled the garage walls with artwork.

Almost imperceptibly at first, I noticed people slowing down and looking at me while I worked in the garage. Then people started to stop and wave. One morning, someone was curious enough to walk up to the garage. They wanted to know about me and what I was doing. It led to an amazing conversation.

Our neighbor, who is from India, stuck his head around the corner one afternoon and asked if I would like to try some Indian food. A caterer by trade, the gentleman was an incredible chef. He would often bring meals over for me and laugh when my face melted off from the spiciness of the food. It was a beautiful connection between two human beings from two very different backgrounds, faiths, and otherwise. He was also much older than me. Yet, we connected with food and laughter.

One time he brought a gift for me. Before I opened it, he said that his family used these in their home, and he thought we might enjoy having one in ours. I couldn't imagine what it was that he was giving us! He told me not to wait any longer, so I excitedly ripped into the package.

I laughed when I saw what was inside the box.

It was a bidet.

I am not kidding you. Our neighbor gave us a bidet as a gift.

Now that is a deep connection.

INVITATION

You are invited to create an old-school paper chain out of construction paper—and if you are feeling extra crafty, you can do it with strips of fabric or other material.

This exercise will help you to explore the different connections in your life.

To make a paper chain, cut paper into several narrow strips of equal length and width. If you want to make it look more interesting, use paper with different colors and patterns.

On each strip of paper, I invite you to write the name of a person, place, thing, or action that is a part of your life. You will then link each strip together by folding the first strip into a ring and then fastening the ends together with tape, glue, or a staple.

Once you have completed your chain, hang it where you can see it over time. Drape it around your bathroom mirror or in your office or studio.

Reflect on these different connections in your life.

REFLECTION

- How did this classic craft help you to explore the different connections in your life?
- How did this exercise highlight connections you didn't realize you had?
- What about connections that you discovered are missing?

SUPPLICATION

Christ, be with me as I strive for connection.
Christ, be with me.
We are more connected than we've ever been.
And we are less connected than we've ever been.
We live in a world of disconnection.
What we long for is a hand to hold.
A neck to hug.
A story to share.
Bread to break.
Help me to foster the connections in my life.
Help me to build new connections.
Christ, be with me as I strive for connection.
Christ, be with me.
Amen.

31. Beginning

Christ, be with me as I begin again. Christ, be with me.

We are currently in a place of perpetual trauma.

I feel it. I feel it from my head to my heart to my toes. I feel it in the interactions I have with those around me. There is a weariness in my human siblings. A palpable grief in the way their bodies move. Shoulders and hearts burdened by so much pain and sadness.

I weep for the murdered children of Sandy Hook and Uvalde. I weep for the millions of people impacted by the wrath and destruction of recent hurricanes. I weep for the division, anger, and injustice sweeping through this country. And I weep for those impacted by the senseless and brutal massacres that take place far too often.

The grief is simply too much to bear—and for many of us, there is a numbness. All of humanity weeps right now, and the fires are burning. Indeed, there is much pain in our world. And we carry much of it on our shoulders and in our hearts.

During Covid, I came up with a word encompassing how I felt: *soul-weary.*

Twenty-five years ago, I took a pottery class from Terri Godfrey at Warren Wilson College in Swannanoa, North Carolina, and created several items, most of them not very memorable. I recently rediscovered one of the vases, took it in my hands, and much to my surprise, I began to weep. Grief washed over me like a waterfall. I cried with my entire being, cradling the vase close to me as if to protect it from breaking like my heart.

Until recently, most of my pottery was with my mom and dad. You know . . . the place where artwork you create as a child ends up. It either clutters the surface of the refrigerator, ends up in a box under a bed somewhere, or like this vase, sits on the shelf in a guest room and collects dust.

Still, I remember the sensation of the wet clay in my hands. I remember the sound of the potter's wheel as it hummed below me. I remember the feeling of the spinning lump of earth in my hands. I remember watching with awe (and some disappointment) as it began to look like an ashtray . . . then a bowl . . . and finally a "vase," a word I use in the most generous sense.

I removed it from the wheel and waited for it to dry. Days passed. Then, I applied the glaze, which is uninspiring before it is fired—dull and thick. I had no idea what it would ultimately look like. It certainly wasn't beautiful in its current form!

We dug a hole in the ground and filled it with sawdust, paper, and leaves. We buried the pot in those same combustibles and set it on fire. After a full day of exposure to intense heat, we covered the pottery and burning material with sand. This last step gives the finished pieces more color and variation

This clay vessel, created by human hands, was returned to earth from where it came. It was transformed by fire and carries scars and burn marks on its surface. Wounds that heal but never go away. The dull glaze now sparkles in the sunlight—a cobalt blue "drip" spills over from the top edge. Blue . . . like the grief that overflows from our eyes and our souls.

Tiny cracks dance across its surface. The vessel will hold, and our colors will shine brighter than before. And we must carry this color and light out into the world.

Let's begin right now.[1]

—————

Maybe you have seen the meme that says "The beginning is near." I absolutely love this message. It reminds me that I don't have to be stuck in the past. Old patterns can change. I can love myself, maybe for the first time.

When I experienced my mental health crisis in 2017, I thought my life was over. I thought I had reached the end. I thought I was going to die.

My truth is that in the ending of what was, I found the beginning of what will be. Maybe this is what they call grace?

To live is to begin again. I find this freeing and life-giving.

I no longer make New Year's resolutions. Why would I, when I never find success, only failure? There is pressure to lose weight, make more money, and look younger. Instead of a New Year's resolution, I choose a word to meditate on. This practice has become more and more common. One of my recent words was "pause." Reflecting on the word "pause" helps me to slow down. It grounds me and helps me to be in the moment. It calms my mind and my soul.

A new beginning doesn't discount the past. In fact, a new beginning is like a well-tended flower garden. The soil is rich with history and experience. The soil is rich with death and resurrection. Seeds are planted in this soil, and in time, the flowers bloom.

Christ, be with me as I begin again. Christ, be with me.

Conclusion

The Art of Calm

As I sit here at my desk, I am overjoyed that the rains have finally returned to Texas.

We are in record-breaking stages of drought. It hasn't been this bad for a very long time. I enjoy hearing the rain fall and the thunder booming. The park where I walk each day—the same place where I search for elusive warblers, and even more elusive peace and calm, is certainly soaking it up.

I worry about the animals that this drought has impacted. Where are the fish? What about the turtles and alligators? The lake once full and teeming with life is dry and looks like the surface of the moon.

I rejoice as the rains fall.

How does one conclude a book like the one you now hold in your hands? I never imagined I would write a book like *The Art of Calm*. I never imagined that the soil of my spirit-filled and colorful life would dry up and crack like the lake where I walk. I thought my brain, heart, and soul were broken beyond repair. But that simply wasn't the case.

One day, while out photographing the dry lakebed, I witnessed nine spectacular white-tailed deer walk out onto land that was once under water. These creatures—majestic and strong—are a community of animals who rely on each other, not only for nurture, but for safety. As I continued to lament the impact of the drought, I began hearing birdsong I had never heard before. Where I saw death, there was life. Even as the lake dried up, new kinds of life appeared. There were different kinds of birds. Deer, raccoon, possums, bobcats, and more were seen walking on the lake bottom. Sparrows of all kinds filled the air with their songs.

I give thanks for the dry lakebed and for the falling rain. I am now able to give thanks for the times when my spirit dries up and I thirst for more. I give thanks for the hard days. And I give thanks for the days I feel like singing.

No one is perfect. Having this awareness gives me wings to soar.

––––––––––––

I have shared some of the most intimate and personal moments of my life. I pray it helps someone. Even one person. Sure, there will certainly be someone who picks this book up, flips through the pages, and doesn't find it very helpful, and that's OK. There might also be someone who picks it up and feels that the book is too self-serving or focused on me, the author. Maybe that is true.

I do know I've given it my best. I've written from the deepest and most pain-filled places in my soul. I certainly can't claim to be master in the art of calm. Still, in the sharing of our stories, we become hope-bearers, truth-tellers, and our lives are transformed. Through creativity and artistic expression, we feel lighter and more hopeful.

When we move our bodies, we experience renewal. And when we weep, the dry bed of our souls experiences renewal.

I still have anxiety. I still have an occasional panic attack. I still have ADHD. I always will, but they are no longer in charge. They do not run my life, nor are they going to run yours.

This book is my gift to you. We can do the hard work, and we can do it together.

———————

Earlier, I wrote about my love of The Order of Compline.

As I finish here, I want to do so with the words of the four collects that are a part of Compline. A collect is simply a prayer meant to gather the intentions of the people and the focus of worship into a succinct prayer.

These are found on page 133 in The Book of Common Prayer:

1. Be our light in the darkness, O Lord, and in your great mercy defend us from all perils and dangers of this night; for the love of your only Son, our Savior Jesus Christ. *Amen.*
2. Be present, O merciful God, and protect us through the hours of this night, so that we who are wearied by the changes and chances of this life may rest in your eternal changelessness; through Jesus Christ our Lord. *Amen.*
3. Look down, O Lord, from your heavenly throne and illumine this night with your celestial brightness; that by night as by day your people may glorify your holy Name; through Jesus Christ our Lord. *Amen.*
4. Visit this place, O Lord, and drive far from it all snares of the enemy; let your holy angels dwell with us to preserve us in peace; and let your blessing be upon us always; through Jesus Christ our Lord. *Amen.*[1]

Acknowledgments

When you have ADHD like I do, writing has significant challenges. Writing an entire book with ADHD is an entirely different ballgame. And I did it!

But not alone.

To my wife, Kristin: You live this story with me, and you save my life every day. You love me deeply and completely. You are my rock, and I love you.

To my daughter, Riley: I stand in awe of you, Ri. I am one lucky dad. I'll love you forever and always. Remember that.

To my parents, in-laws, and extended family: Thank you for loving me. I love you more.

To my agent, Keely Boeving: Thank you for saying "Yes." We make a good team!

To the remarkable team at Church Publishing Incorporated—especially my editor, Phil Marino: Thank you for sticking with me—and sticking it to me. You have made this a better book, and me a better writer.

To my friend Jared Johnson: It's "Cemetery-Time" somewhere! I love you, friend.

To my good buddies Jack and Jim: It's your turn to pick where we are going to lunch. My treat.

To Sasha and Sally: You sat with me. I will never forget it.

To the Episcopal Church: Expansive, challenging, and inspiring.

To Neil, Ryan, Liz, David, Sue, Tara, Jessica, Dustin, Brady, Ken, Gerry, Jimmy, Clarence, Heidi, and Mike: I can't imagine a better team to serve with.

To all my Palmer friends and family.

To my Trinity Cathedral friends.

To my Warren Wilson College family.

To my Kanuga Camps & Conferences family.

To my photography and birding family.

To Cullinan Park Nature Conservancy.

To my Sony RX10iv camera.

To my manuscript readers: Kristin Hutchison, Sandy and Hal Hutchison (Mom and Dad, of course), Rebecca Yu, Kelly Soika, and Keith Hall—thank you.

RECIPE FOR CHARLIE BROWNS

INGREDIENTS

1 stick unsalted butter
½ cup whole milk
2 cups granulated sugar
¾ cup peanut butter
1 teaspoon vanilla extract
3½ cups quick-cooking oats

INSTRUCTIONS

1. Bring butter, milk, and sugar to a boil. Boil for 1 to 2 minutes.
2. Remove from heat.
3. Add ¾ cup peanut butter and stir. Add vanilla flavoring.
4. Add 3½ cups of quick cooking oats.
5. Drop by spoonful onto wax paper and let cool.

Notes

1. CRASH

1. W. Zheng, "Algorithm of Flood Monitoring and Analysis Based on SMAP Data," 2019 IEEE 8th Joint International Information Technology and Artificial Intelligence Conference (ITAIC), 2019, pp. 911–14, doi: 10.1109/ITAIC.2019.8785459.

3. FEAR

1. Kendra Cherry, "What Is Mood?" Verywell Mind, August 2, 2022, https://www.verywellmind.com/what-is-mood-5271921.
2. Saprea.org, "Kintsugi: The Value of a Broken Bowl," The Younique Foundation, https://youniquefoundation.org/kintsugi-the-value-of-a-broken-bowl/? (accessed January 9, 2023).
3. Roger Hutchison, "Since September 11th . . . ," The Episcopal Church and Visual Arts, September 22, 2001, https://ecva.org/exhibition/sincesept11/pages/hutchison.html.

5. ANXIETY

1. "Warren Wilson College Recognizes Outstanding Alumni at Homecoming," Warren Wilson College, October 17, 2017, https://www.warren-wilson.edu/2017/10/18/warren-wilson-college-recognizes-outstanding-alumni-homecoming/.

7. REMEMBER

1. This story comes from my book *Jesus: God Among Us* (Church Publishing, 2018).

8. MARKED

1. Katelyn Wilde, "Bluebird Symbolism and Spiritual Meaning," Sonoma Birding, https://www.sonomabirding.com/bluebird-symbolism/ (accessed January 9, 2023).

2. Hood Construction, "Trinity Episcopal Cathedral," https://www.hood-construction.com/portfolio/trinity-episcopal-cathedral/ (accessed January 9, 2023).

9. ANGER

1. Robert B. Kruschwitz, ed., *Anger*, Christian Reflection: A Series in Faith and Ethics, The Institute for Faith and Learning, Baylor University, https://www.baylor.edu/content/services/document.php/235693.pdf (accessed January 9, 2022).
2. "22 Empath Quotes: Beyond Just Being Sensitive," The Goal Chaser, https://thegoalchaser.com/empath-quotes/ (accessed January 9, 2023).
3. Marcus Mund and Kristin Mitte, "The Costs of Repression: A Meta-Analysis on the Relation between Repressive Coping and Somatic Diseases," National Library of Medicine, September 2012, https://pubmed.ncbi.nlm.nih.gov/22081940/; Crystal Raypole, "Let It Out: Dealing with Repressed Emotions," Healthline, March 31, 2020, http://healthline.com/health/repressed-emotions#physical-effects.
4. Geraldine Walsh, "Fears for Tears: Why Do We Tell Boys Not to Cry," *Irish Times,* September 10, 2019, https://www.irishtimes.com/life-and-style/health-family/parenting/fears-for-tears-why-do-we-tell-boys-not-to-cry-1.4006399.

13. SEE

1. Angela Nelson, "Synesthesia," medically reviewed by Christopher Melinosky, MD, WebMD, https://www.webmd.com/brain/what-is-synesthesia (accessed January 9, 2023).
2. Vincent van Gogh, *The Letters of Vincent van Gogh* (Touchstone, repr. ed., 2008).
3. David Foster Wallace, commencement speech, Kenyon College, 2005; full transcript available at Farnham Street, https://fs.blog/david-foster-wallace-this-is-water/ (accessed January 9, 2023).
4. Robert Henri, *The Art Spirit* (Philadelphia: J. B. Lippincott, 1923).

14. LISTEN

1. Richard Rohr, *Everything Belongs: The Gift of Contemplative Prayer*, rev. and updated ed. (New York: Crossroad, 2003).

15. GROW

1. Elisabeth Johnson, "Fifth Sunday of Easter," Working Preacher, May 15, 2022, https://www.workingpreacher.org/commentaries/revised-common

-lectionary/fifth-sunday-of-easter-3/commentary-on-john-1331-35-5 (accessed January 9, 2023).
2. BCP, 283.
3. Roger Hutchison, *My Favorite Color is Blue. Sometimes.: A Journey Through Loss with Art and Color* (Paraclete Press, 2017), 22.

16. TRUTH

1. Adam Kirsch, "Søren Kierkegaard's Struggle with Himself," *The New Yorker*, May 4, 2020, https://www.newyorker.com/magazine/2020/05/11 /soren-kierkegaards-struggle-with-himself (accessed January 9, 2023).

17. HOLY

1. "Hans Hofmann: The Artist," Hans Hofmann, http://www.hanshofmann. org/about (accessed January 9, 2023).

18. STRONG

1. Robin Marantz Henig, "Understanding the Anxious Mind," *New York Times*, September 29, 2009, https://www.nytimes.com/2009/10/04/magazine /04anxiety-t.html.
2. This story is dedicated to Christopher D'Olier Reeve, an American actor, best recognized for playing the titular character in the film *Superman* and its first three sequels. Although Christopher is most famous for his role as Superman, a role which he played with both charisma and grace, his acting career spans a much larger ground. Paralyzed after a horse-riding accident, he died suddenly at age fifty-two after several years of living and working with his severe disability. Originally published as the following blog post: Roger Hutchison, "Reflection: Have We Turned God into Superman?" Building Faith, June 27, 2013, https://buildfaith.org/superman/?.

22. PRAYER

1. Oxford English Dictionary.

23. HOPE

1. Polly Campbell, "Why Hope Matters," *Psychology Today*, February 5, 2019, https://www.psychologytoday.com/us/blog/imperfect-spirituality/201902 /why-hope-matters.

26. COLOR

1. Originally published as the following blog post: Roger Hutchison, "Light and Love," Episcopal News Service, May 13, 2013, https://www.episcopal newsservice.org/pressreleases/light-and-love/.

2. Originally published as the following blog post: Roger Hutchison, "Baptism," Baptized for Life, https://baptizedforlife.org/baptism/ (accessed January 9, 2023).

28. RITUAL

1. BCP, 127–35.

29. PURPOSE

1. Ikigai Tribe, "Find Your Ikigai," https://ikigaitribe.com/ikigai/ikigai-worksheet/ (accessed January 9, 2023).

31. BEGINNING

1. Originally published as the following blog post: Roger Hutchison, "Surprised by Grief," Paraclete Press, October 4, 2017, https://paracletepress.com/blogs/paraclete-press-blog/surprised-by-grief.

CONCLUSION. THE ART OF CALM

1. BCP, 133.

LIST OF MENTAL
HEALTH RESOURCES

ASSOCIATIONS AND GENERAL
MENTAL HEALTH RESOURCES

American Counseling Association https://www.counseling.org/
American Psychological Association https://www.apa.org/
HealthyPlace—America's Mental Health Channel
    https://www.healthyplace.com
NAMI (National Alliance on Mental Illness) https://nami.org/
National Institute of Mental Health https://www.nimh.nih.gov/
National Mental Health Association http://www.nmha.org/
National Women's Health Resource Center
    https://www.healthywomen.org/
Substance Abuse and Mental Health Services Administration
    https://www.samhsa.gov/
World Federation for Mental Health https://www.wfmh.org/

SUICIDE AWARENESS AND HOTLINES

American Foundation for Suicide Prevention https://afsp.org/
National Suicide Prevention Hotline https://www.imalive.org/
Suicide Awareness Voices of Education https://save.org/
Suicide: Read This First - https://metanoia.org/suicide/

DEPRESSION AND MOOD DISORDERS

Coping with Depression https://www.helpguide.org/articles
/depression/dealing-with-depression-during-coronavirus.htm

Depression and Bipolar Support Alliance (DBSA)
https://www.dbsalliance.org/

Depression and How Therapy Can Help https://www.apa.org
/topics/depression/recover

Depression Marathon https://depressionmarathon.blogspot
.com/#axzz7pd8mMG00

Freedom From Fear https://www.freedomfromfear.org/

ANXIETY

Answers to Your Questions About Panic Disorder
https://www.apa.org/topics/anxiety/panic-disorder

Anxiety and Depression Association of America https://adaa.org/

Anxiety Guru http://www.anxietyguru.net/

Anxiety: How to Clear Your Head When Worry Sets In https://
www.helpguide.org/articles/anxiety/how-to-stop-worrying.htm

The Anxiety Network https://anxietynetwork.com/

Anxiety Slayer https://www.anxietyslayer.com/

Positively Positive https://www.positivelypositive.com/

Social Anxiety Disorder https://www.verywellmind.com/
social-anxiety-disorder-4157220

OBSESSIVE-COMPULSIVE DISORDER (OCD)

Beyond OCD https://beyondocd.org/

International OCD Foundation https://iocdf.org/

Obsessive Compulsive Information Center https://miminc.org/

POST-TRAUMATIC STRESS DISORDER (PTSD)

Give an Hour for Veterans and Their Families
https://giveanhour.org/
National Center for PTSD https://www.ptsd.va.gov/
Real Warriors (U.S. Department of Defense) (for
veterans and their families) https://www.health.
mil/Military-Health-Topics/Centers-of-Excellence/
Psychological-Health-Center-of-Excellence/
Real-Warriors-Campaign
Sidran Institute http://www.sidran.org/

PRENATAL/POSTPARTUM MENTAL HEALTH

Depression After Delivery https://www.womenshealth
.gov/mental-health/mental-health-conditions/
postpartum-depression
Women of Color Health Equity Collective http://wochec.org/
My Postpartum Voice http://www.mypostpartumvoice.com/
Postpartumdepression.org
Postpartum Health Alliance https://postpartumhealthalliance.org/
Postpartum Progress https://postpartumprogress.com/
Postpartum Stress Center https://postpartumstress.com/
Postpartum Support International https://www.postpartum.net/
Seleni Institute https://www.seleni.org/

GRIEF AND LOSS

The Dougy Center http://www.dougy.org/
National Alliance for Grieving Children https://nacg.org/
Open To Hope https://www.opentohope.com/
Pregnancy and Infant Loss Network https://pailnetwork
.sunnybrook.ca/

The Sweeney Alliance https://sweeneyalliance.org/
Unspoken Grief (Perinatal/Neonatal Loss) http://unspokengrief
.com/

RELATIONSHIPS AND INTIMACY

The Relationship Institute http://www.therelationshipinstitute.org/

TEENS

LGBT National Help Center for Youth https://www.lgbthotline
.org/
iFred https://www.ifred.org/
NIDA for teens https://nida.nih.gov/
To Write Love on Her Arms https://twloha.com/

LIST OF CHILDREN'S BOOKS

After the Fall by Dan Santat
Beautiful Oops! by Barney Saltzberg
Be Kind by Pat Zietlow Miller
The Big Umbrella by Amy June Bates
Courage by Bernard Waber
The Day You Begin by Jacqueline Woodson
Enemy Pie by Derek Munson
Going Places by Paul A. Reynolds
Grumpy Monkey by Susanne Lang
I Am Human: A Book of Empathy by Susan Verde
I Am Love: A Book of Compassion by Susan Verde
I'm NOT Just a Scribble by Diane Alber
The Invisible Boy by Trudy Ludwig
ish by Peter H. Reynolds
Love by Matt de la Peña
Mama, Do You Love Me? by Barbara M. Jooss
The Most Magnificent Thing by Ashley Spires
My Favorite Color Is Blue. Sometimes. by Roger Hutchison
One by Kathryn Otashi
Perfect Square by Michael Hall
Ricky, the Rock That Couldn't Roll by Jay Miletsky
Seeds and Trees: A Children's Book about the Power of Words by
 Brandon Walden
We're All Wonders by R. J. Palacio
What Do You Do With . . . (series) by Kobi Yamada
Wherever You Are: My Love Will Find You by Nancy Tillman

CPSIA information can be obtained
at www.ICGtesting.com
Printed in the USA
JSHW021730070523
41370JS00004B/5